Simon & Schuster's Guide to
CATS

by Gino Pugnetti
Mordecai Siegal, U.S. Editor

A FIRESIDE BOOK
PUBLISHED BY SIMON & SCHUSTER INC.
New York London Toronto Sydney Tokyo Singapore

Copyright © 1983 by Arnoldo Mondadori S.p.A. Milano
English language translation copyright © 1983 by Arnoldo Mondadori
Editore, S.p.A. Milano

A Fireside Book
Published by Simon & Schuster, Inc.
Simon & Schuster Building
Rockefeller Center
1230 Avenue of the Americas
New York, New York 10020
FIRESIDE and colophon are registered trademarks
of Simon & Schuster, Inc.

Printed in Spain by Artes Gráficas Toledo, S.A.
D.L.TO:17–1995

10 9 8 7 6 5 4 3 2 1
10 9   Pbk.

Library of Congress Cataloging in Publication Data

Pugnetti Gino.
  Simon & Schuster's guide to cats.

  Translation of: Gatti.
  Bibliography: p.
  Includes index.
  1. Cats. I. Siegal, Mordecai. II. Title.
III. Title: Simon and Schuster's guide to cats.
SF442.P8213   1983   636.8   83-13634
ISBN 0-671-49167-9
        0-671-49170-9 Pbk.

---

*The breed descriptions in this book were meant to introduce the
reader to the great variety of coat colors, patterns, and types as
well as body types and characteristics. They delineate the physical
cat from breed to breed, helping the reader to form a mental portrait.
These breed descriptions are not the official standards of the Cat
Fanciers Association, Inc., of the United States (CFA) or the Governing Council of the Cat Fancy of Great Britain (GCCF). However,
in many respects they conform to North American standards, differing in some points of detail from British standards.*

CONTENTS

KEY TO SYMBOLS

Adapts to leash: Although many breeds have a profound dislike for a leash there are those cats, usually the Siamese and other oriental breeds, that can be trained to accept it and look forward to walks.

Needs extra grooming: The long-haired breeds with silky fur and/or woolly undercoats require daily grooming to keep their fur from matting.

Good mouser: The ability to hunt, capture, and kill prey depends on several elements. Often it is the mother that teaches her kittens to hunt. However, there does seem to be a greater instinct to mouse in certain breeds.

Needs vital space: Some breeds are much more rugged or much more active and adventuresome than others. All cats can adapt to indoor life but these more "outgoing" cats would enjoy a romp in the garden.

Long-lived: A longer life expectancy can be predicted for some breeds but, of course, it cannot be guaranteed.

Good with children: Some cats, like some human beings, love to play with and live with children.

Tranquil: Some breeds of cat, such as the Persian/Longhair, are more sedate and less active.

Active indoors: Many breeds of cat, such as the Abyssinian, are happiest when they are doing something. They seem to be always on the go.

Home-loving: The comforts of home are much more appealing than the call of the wild to these felines.

Likes to travel: Although many breeds dislike change, some, especially the oriental-type cats, enjoy traveling and a change of scene.

Very vocal: Siamese cats and breeds related to the Siamese are known for their very audible and expressive sound. They not only have a very distinctive voice, they have quite a bit to say.

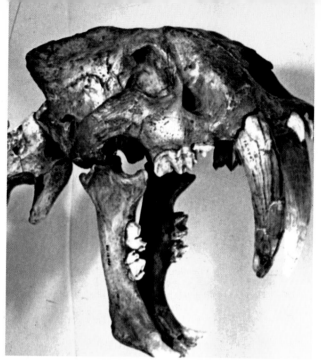
The head of a saber-toothed tiger with its characteristic canines well in view.

The ancient cats of the forest

The cat is the most mysterious and fascinating animal that has ever coexisted with man. Paleontology, the science that studies ancient life forms and animal fossils, even with its modern methods of research, has only been able to offer vague notions on the cat's origin. It has, however, been ascertained that about 50 million years ago a wild animal with a long body and short legs existed. It was named Miacis, the most ancient ancestor of the cat. The first cats lived in forests and were similar to modern martens, which are still sought for their precious fur. These cats were able to climb trees easily and had paws with retractible claws just as cats do today.

Famous among all existing wild feline species were the saber-toothed tigers, forerunners of the cat, named for their sharp, daggerlike canines. With these formidable weapons they were capable of killing a full-grown elephant. Saber-toothed tigers were plentiful in Europe, Asia, Africa, and North America about 35 million years ago, but their small brain (limited intelligence), large body, and cumbersome set of teeth (even though essential to their survival) caused their extinction.

The last to approach man

The oldest fossils that show a similarity to the modern cat date back 10 to 12 million years ago, much earlier than the appearance of man, dog, horse, or pig. These latter animals, today defined as domestic, were immediately taken advantage of by man (i.e., the dog as hunter, horse as transporter, cattle and swine as laborers and sources of milk and meat). Meanwhile, the cat, not useful to anyone, remained master of itself, independent and fierce. It therefore enjoyed a long and free existence. But could man not become fascinated by this beautiful, wild, and magical wanderer? And could the cat remain indifferent to the flatteries of that strange and civilized being that was man? The cat, last in the line of domesticated animals, decided one day to make friends with man. Actually, the relationship came about not out of affection but out of self-interest because the cat could not resist the succulent mice that roamed in the granaries of Egypt. So man did everything to keep such a useful animal.

The cat went from a wild to a domesticated state (a precise date is unknown), but in a noble way of extraordinary and aloof distinction. A hunter of mice, yes, but calm and respectable. It did not accept a dog's lifestyle, occupied with the hunt for 45,000 years, but immediately ingratiated itself in the court of kings.

The oldest known evidence of an urban cat was found in an Egyptian tomb of 4,500 years ago. The domestic cat, as we know it today, is a modern animal. Neither the Antarctic nor Australia can boast of native cats. The wild species of cats arrived in South America by the phenomenon of the continental drift. South America joined North America only 2 million years ago, thus permitting the cat's emigration.

In the meantime, nature did not remain inactive. In Australia there appeared the Marsupialia, which comprised many species similar to the cat and occupied the same evolutionary niche. It could almost be said that if cats had not existed then, nature would have evolved them at another time.

A glance at the ferocious relatives

All felines are classified not only by many common anatomical characteristics but also by particular cellular affinity. Almost all felines have thirty-eight chromosomes in every cell.

The classification of felines is not easy, however. One characteristic, important for classification, is the structure of the hyoid bone, which is partially made of cartilage in the lion, tiger, leopard, and cheetah. This enables the vocal apparatus to move freely so that these wild beasts can roar. In other felines the hyoid bone is rigid and so impedes roaring. Felines in general walk on their toes, which allows them to run faster than if they were to walk on the flat of their paws.

They have well-developed hearing and sight, which enable them to discover prey at dawn and twilight, unlike other carnivorous animals. Their sense of smell is not used for hunting but is important for detecting the presence of other animals.

The coloring of a wild cat's coat has evolved in such a way as to disguise the cat in the face of its prey. The spotted cats, such as the leopard and cheetah, are only found in the forest. Stripes hide the tiger in any prairie or jungle. The lion, with its sandy color, lives in the African savannah. Some felines, like the leopard, have an almost black coat that hides them in the dark. White tigers with blue eyes also exist.

Wild felines are found all over the world except in the tundra and the polar regions. They lead an inactive life, interrupted by excursions to find food. They can devour prey one-third the size of their weight, and once satiated do not eat again for a week. They often sleep eighteen hours a day, stirring only when they are hungry. In this respect the domestic cat is very similar to its wild relatives.

Panthera leo. A large male lion measures to 9 feet long, 3 feet tall at the shoulder. He weighs between 400 and 500 pounds.

Bestiary table of the eighteenth century. From the domestic cat to the tiger and lion, the cats are depicted with respect to their actual proportions.

Most felines are loners. Lions, which usually live in familial packs with one leader, are the exception. In other species males and females live together only for reproduction: females make known to males that they are ready to mate by leaving a trail of urine within their territory.

The tiger is the largest and most infamous relative of the cat. The male can be 11.5 feet (3.5 meters) long (tail included), 4.5 feet (1.4 meters) tall, and weigh 600 pounds (300 kg.). It is nicknamed "man-eater." In fact, in the mid-1800s, tigers consumed 400 human victims a year in Singapore alone. Tigers and lions are very similar to each other. When they are skinned, they are no longer anatomically distinguishable. They can mate and produce cubs that in turn reproduce.

The cheetah is a large and easily tamable cat that is not a man-eater. Once in captivity, and with proper environmental conditions, it may come to care for its owner, respond to calls and orders, and can be taken for a walk on a leash. It is very fast and can reach a velocity of up to 60 miles (90 km.) per hour. Other felines include the leopard, panther, cougar, and lynx.

Triumphal march in Egypt
Scientists seem to agree that the domestic cat is a cross between the Felis sylvestris [or European Wildcat] and the Felis lybica [or African Wildcat], and that it belongs to the mammal class, carnivorous order, Felidae family, Felis genus, and Felis catus species. Of the great Felidae family, it is the only one to have accepted to live in man's house. It is therefore just to baptize it with the scientific name Felis domestica.

Before becoming domesticated, the cat paid for its freedom by suffering hunger and the cold and living by sanguineous plunder like a small

Lynx Rufus (bobcat).

tiger. It would never sell itself to man for a piece of meat or the warmth of a fire. Only in the third millennium B.C. did it concede, beginning its domestic future. In the Egyptian courts the cat was loved and deified. The Egyptians believed that some divinities assumed the semblance of a cat, and so the high priests decreed divine orders and omens of the future according to its behavior.

The tendency to deify animals already existed in ancient Egypt, so the cat found a fertile terrain for its career. Priests previously directed their sacred attentions to the lion, but since it was a ferocious and cumbersome animal, as soon as the cat was discovered they opted for it. Even if not completely tame, it was at least more manageable. Also, as new generations appeared, it was noticed that they were tamer and allowed themselves to be caressed by the human hand. The cat was now a unique animal with fascinating movements and statuary poses.

The "mau" enter the house
Sacred, and therefore venerated, the cat slowly began to enter homes and accept the company of humans. They were also grateful to the cat because it freed the granaries of mice, which were coming from the Nile. The cat meows, so the Egyptians named it "mau."

The goddess of the cat head
The first official consecration of the cat in North Africa took place when the Egyptian goddess Bast, the symbol of fecundity and beauty, was depicted with the head of a cat and a mysterious, bewitching glance. Another name given to this goddess was Pasht. The diminutive "puss" may derive from this name.

(box) An ancient Egyptian painting depicting a cat on a leash and a full plate of food.

This beautiful goddess was the symbol of light, heat, and solar energy. Depicted as a cat, mysterious and lover of the night, she was also the symbol of the moon. It was also believed that she controlled the fertility of man and beast, cured illnesses, and watched over the souls of the dead. It is therefore understandable why the pharaohs' laws so rigorously defended a cat's life. Whoever killed a cat faced the possibility of being condemned to death.

A Roman dignitary, who accidently killed a cat in Egypt, was barely saved from a lynching by an exasperated population. Cats usually died a natural death and enjoyed a burial with the honors of state.

Three hundred thousand mummies

The pharaohs also considered cows, serpents, and fish sacred. For this reason, Egyptians were vegetarians for many centuries. But the "mau" always remained the most sacred animal. The worship and care for its well-being was scrupulously passed on from father to son. At the divine animal's death, the embalming was taken care of and the owners grieved as they would for a member of the family. The wealthier the family, the more elaborate the sarcophagus. Embalmed mice were placed next to the cat. This Egyptian period was probably the most serene, calm, and refined for the cat.

Over 300,000 cat mummies were uncovered in 1890 in one of the ancient capitals of Egypt. They were still enclosed in their cases of engraved wood or wrapped in colored, intertwined straw, and wrapped in rich bandages of various colors. The faces were covered by masks on which the nose, eyes, ears, and whiskers were evident.

Hunting scene from the tomb of Menes, 3000 B.C., Thebes.

Some of these historical cat mummies were distributed among the museums of the world. But there were so many that the better part of the "sacred corpses" were later used as an excellent fertilizer, like the mud of the Nile, perhaps even better.

In 595 B.C., the Persians were unsuccessfully besieging Pelusia, a city on the Egyptian border. King Cambise, son of Cyrus the Great, had the idea of furnishing each of his 600 soldiers with a cat. The boorish army attached the venerated animals onto their battle shields, and the Egyptians no longer dared to counterattack for fear of hitting one of the cats. That was how Pelusia was conquered by the Persians.

The worship of Bast gradually began to decline after 350 A.D., and was completely lost and forgotten after the imperial decree in 390 A.D. Many Egyptian murals remain that depict cats participating in family life. One noted painting exhibited at the British Museum in London shows a large, striped cat accompanying a man on a hunting expedition, holding down two birds with its paws and snatching another with its mouth.

The landing in Europe
The only mouse-hunters in ancient Europe were semi-domesticated weasels and skunks—not very pleasant animals. The skunk was a particularly unappealing companion. The Greeks were the first, during their commercial dealings with the Egyptians, to discover another animal that was not only a great mouse-hunter but also beautiful, refined, clean, and best of all, not smelly.

The Egyptians, even with the pressing requests of the Greeks, would not make their god an object of commercial exchange. The Greeks,

probably by some deception of which the history of mankind is rich, stole at least six pairs of cats and transported them back to Greece.

After two months the first litters were born, and after a few years the breeders were in a position to sell the cats to the Romans, Gauls, and Celts. The proverbial prolificity of cats took care of the rest and, in the new lands, the mice, plunderers of granaries and carriers of disease, suffered their first defeats.

Cats became popular in Europe in the first century after Christ when the unfailing chronicler Pliny the Elder described their physical characteristics in his *Natural History*. It seems that the independent qualities of the cat were valued quite highly by the Romans since the cat was appointed the symbol of liberty.

A friend of the Buddhists

With good commercial relations existing between Asia and Europe, the cat was exchanged for pure silk, and thus arrived in China. The cat met with success even there; in addition to being a destroyer of mice, it was raised to symbolize peace, fortune, and family serenity because of its beauty. Even today, in some Asiatic sanctuaries, divine powers are attributed to the cat, and it is believed that in the hereafter its soul speaks to Buddha in favor of the owner that still lives on earth.

Small ceramic statues of Asiatic cats remain as testimony to how highly the feline was regarded, to the degree that behind their hollow eyes small oil lamps were lit so that the mice might imagine that their enemies were awake and ready to catch them. The cat's power to see in the dark was also considered useful to hold evil spirits at bay; since

The Birman cat descends from cats that were venerated as gods in the Buddhist temples. The priests believed that the faithful returned to earth in the form of a cat.

Chinese merchants of cats showing their animals to clients.

it was usually thought that they were more active at night, the walls of many Asiatic houses were adorned with images of cats.

The older and more hairless the house cat was, the greater the fortune the cat would bring to its owners according to legend.

Much appreciated by the Buddhists was the cat's capacity for meditation, which they sensed in the animals. Yet the cat doesn't appear on the list of animals protected in the original canons of Buddhism. This exclusion is owed to an accident that happened to a cat when it was not very involved in its duty: it fell asleep while the solemn funeral ceremony of Buddha was taking place.

Cats landed in India at the same time as in China. The feline divinity named Sastht, the symbol of maternity, is comparable to the Egyptian goddess Bast. It is a rule in the Hindu religion to host or at least feed a cat. Cats were introduced to Japan from China in the Middle Ages. According to legend, the first Japanese cats appeared in 999 in the imperial palace of Kyoto. From that moment, great treatment and honorable attention were paid to the beautiful feline, nourished and fondled to the same degree as were the famous lapdogs. But the result of this excessively genteel treatment was that the unhunted mice proliferated. The mice began to multiply at an alarming speed, and to fight them the Japanese painted and sculpted images of ferocious felines on the walls of their houses. It was only much later, perhaps in the seventeenth century, that Japanese cats were allowed to hunt freely according to their instinct, having been spoiled for centuries by caresses and delicacies.

The cat crossed over from Egypt to the Arabian countries of Islam, where the revered animal was the horse. But the popularity of the cat grew to equal, if not surpass with intensity, the fame of the horse.

Even Muhammad owned a cat, a female named Muezza. A legend with an authentic flavor is told that one day Muezza was napping on the couch next to the prophet, who having to get up but not wanting to disturb the sleep of his beloved cat, preferred to cut off a piece of his *gellaba* on which the animal was stretched.

Evil cats at the stake

Contact with civilization was a fortunate success for the cat, which lasted some millennia. But the mood of the world can suddenly change, and after a long period of love between man and cat there began a dramatic era that history cannot overlook.

The Church began to frown on the adoration directed toward the cat and considered it an animal too compromised with paganism. Persecution was exercised in degrees because Saint Patrick in the fifth century, and Pope Gregory Magro a century after, affectionately reared many cats, and they were also depicted in paintings of Saint Agatha and Saint Gertrude. The monasteries were the first Christian communities to benefit from the cat's instinct of hunting mice. The Celtic monks, in particular, were active breeders of cats. An Irish priest's poem remains, which was dedicated to a white cat, his faithful friend.

At the beginning of the Middle Ages, the cat was still tolerated, and in many cases protected and loved by the people. Its capacity as a killer of mice was admired as always by owners of stables and warehouses. General respect for the cat grew, however, when Europe was invaded by squadrons of dreadful black rats, devourers of cereal and fruit. Coming from the East, they arrived hidden in the holds of ships from the end of the eleventh century. It became immediately clear that the only answer to the dramatic problem was the intervention en masse of an army of warlike cats.

In the Middle Ages, at the moment when rat extermination was becoming urgently necessary to the point of removing them en masse, the cat became the personification of an evil witch. While in Egypt the cat was raised to symbolize a god, it now plunged to hell and became a demon. The hostility began in the middle of the thirteenth century. It seems to have been provoked by the return to the adoration of a Norwegian divinity, Freya, pagan goddess of fertility. The cat played a part in the rites of this divinity.

To combat the cat divinity with all the rigors of an inquisition, the Church authorized a total persecution of the cat. The cat is never even mentioned in the Bible. This irrational condemnation was easily passed on to a fanatical people. But the superstition also reached the nobility, and the poor cat, in every way, was taken as the source of all evil.

In Mary Tudor's England, the cat was burned as a sign of heresy of Protestantism, and under the reign of Elizabeth I as the symbol of Catholic heresy. It was also widely believed that witches were able to transform themselves into cats, and was thus yet another motive to continue with the inhumane massacre.

The inquisition resulted in one common bonfire of heretics, witches, assassins, and cats. The people committed dishonorable atrocities. The festival of Saint John on June 24 remained infamous: in many town squares, grates were raised upon which cats, captured by the people, were thrown. Their end came as they burned amidst the hysterical cries of a crowd that felt itself liberated from the devil's evil influence. So this tortured and killed animal, certainly by no fault of its own, was missing at the tragic appointment with the plague. The species was almost extinct in 1400, and there wasn't a sufficient number of cats to kill the rats, which were carrying the infectious bubonic fleas. For lack of cats, two-thirds of the European population died of the plague.

The false beliefs and cruelties lasted a few centuries, solicited not only by the men of the Church but by sovereigns and princes. It was thanks to Louis XIV, king of France, that the terrible ceremonies in the squares were prohibited, and only after the French Revolution were they almost completely considered superstitions and cruelties.

Louis Pasteur, with his scientific discoveries in the mid-1800s, was responsible for renewing the positive feelings toward the cat. People began to understand the nature of illness and its transmissibility (by microbes, not witches), and saw in cats a perfect public example of hygiene: animals that "cleaned" themselves twenty times a day.

If anyone today still believes in the evil of cats (and there are many superstitions concerning them), it's the last trace of ancient fears and superstitions.

"Qato" in all the world

After having been called "mau" in Upper Egypt, the word "qato" from the Syrian was coined for the cat. This seems to be the true root of the diminutive "gatto." Another possible derivation may be from the Latin adjective "cautus," intended as astute; or from the French "guetter," with the significance of spying, as the cat is always active with its eyes and ears. It may be a question of etymological fantasy, given that the use of "qato" in Egypt appears centuries before the felines spread to Athens, Rome, or Gaul.

In any case, it may certainly be said that it comes from a unique root, whether from the Syrian origin (qato) or late Latin (cattus), or Arabic (quett). These bases then serve to identify the cat in many languages but with slight modification. Unlike the word for dog, which is defined by many different sounds (dog, chien, hund, pierro, etc.), the word for cat is chat in French, katze in German, gato in Spanish, katta in Swedish, kat in Dutch and Danish, and so on.

Literature and cats

Two great fabulists of the past had recounted very pleasant stories about the cat. The first was Aesop, the Greek fabulist of the sixth century B.C., who preached stinging morals about the animal-man relationship. Many centuries later the Latin writer Fedro modernized the style and philosophy of Aesop's fables. After Aesop, the Greek historian Herodotus (480 B.C.), the Roman orator Cicero (106 B.C.), and the indefatigable chronicler Pliny the Elder (23 B.C.) wrote about the cat. In their wake, many other minor writers wrote beautiful, elegiac, and striking pages about the feline.

But after the fall of the Roman Empire, during the notorious anti-cat period of the Middle Ages, even the lesser writers proportioned their changing views toward the negative fashion of the time, either out of fear of being unpopular or lack of inspiration. From that period there exists rhymes of love for God and women, but there is no literary writing of worth concerning the cat. The goodness of Saint Francis toward animals was a pale light isolated only in Umbria, which bore fruit later.

Cats seem to love the silence of libraries, the intimate studies of learned men, the disorder of tables cluttered with paper, the batting of typewriter keys, and napping on a book cover. Working writers enjoy

their company knowing they will be bothered only by a purring of love.

At the beginning of the Renaissance, when the darkness of the Middle Ages was coming to an end, the Italian poet Francesco Petrarch publicly proclaimed his love of cats. This signified the break with the past and its invasion of demons. Retiring to the Euganei Hills near Padua, Petrarch lived the years of his old age in solitude together with a cat and died in 1374, reclining his head on an open book in the comfort of his feline friend. The remains of the cat, in memory of the affection the poet had for it, are preserved in a museum in Padua.

Another Italian poet, Torquato Tasso, in 1590 (already old and in disgrace at the court of Ferrara, almost blind and in such misery that he didn't even have the money to buy lamp oil) wrote an adorable sonnet for his cat, comparing the eyes to two stars and invoking them to give him light on the page to dedicate his last poem to life. Lope de Vega, the sixteenth-century Spanish dramatist, loved cats so much that he even wrote "Gattomachia" (battle among cats), a pompous poem in which the virtues of felines are praised and the defects of man are ridiculed. The fabulists of 1600, with the leading French school La Fontaine, imitators of Aesop and Fedro, followed by Charles Perrault ("Puss in Boots," "Cinderella"), almost always treated cats as characters representing man, demonstrating their defects as well as their hypocrisy, thievery, and laziness. They joked with their pens, speaking of cats while criticizing people.

A learned man of animals, the French naturalist Georges Louis Leclerc de Buffon, who lived in the mid-1700s, accomplished a step backward. In his *Histoire Naturelle* he expressed severe judgment on the cat, defining it "an unfaithful domestic, that we keep only out of necessity," and he referred to the inexhaustible aspect of hunter of mice.

Detail of an etching by William Hogarth, First Phase of Cruelty.

But in his turn, the abbot Ferdincindo Galicani, man of letters, economist, and Italian diplomat at the French court, affirmed that he had never found anyone who had profoundly studied the intimate character of the cat, and that which was written about it was the fruit of supposition and acrimony.

During the eighteenth century a pro-feline cult developed in France. The attitude of zoophilists was shaped by a witty book on cats by the obscure author Paradis de Moncrif. He wrote that if people could withstand a bit of public mockery they would find great comfort for their ideas on the cunningness and intelligence of cats.

In the mid-1800s the French poet Charles Baudelaire, the famous author of the collection of verses "The Flowers of Evil," also discovered the sensuality of the cat. He described what he felt while his fingers caressed its head, the elastic back, the electric body of the female house cat, paralleling these sensations to being in contact with a beautiful woman. These significant verses of Baudelaire read: "Come, my beautiful cat, onto my loving heart—pull back your claws and let me lose myself in your beautiful eyes—medley of sapphire and agate."

Guy de Maupassant, author of short stories and novels in the latter half of the nineteenth century (his last name begins with "mau"), treated the cat rather like a voluptuous being. "I felt against my cheek the hollow and vibrant side in a continual hum, and sometimes, a stretched paw rested on my mouth, five outstretched nails pierced me, then immediately drew back in." It is, however, a familiar gesture known to all cat-owners.

Among the various literary praisers of the cat, Francois René de Châteaubriand (1768–1848) should be remembered for his autobiog-

24

Puss in Boots harangues the farmers. Etching by Gustave Doré.

raphy *Memories Beyond the Grave*, in which he wrote about his contact with a cat as being one of the most important events of his life. Châteaubriand also disputed the obscure theories of the naturalist Georges Louis Leclerc de Buffon—enemy of the cat. This posthumous polemic inspired Pope Leone XII to send Châteaubriand a gift of a magnificent copy of a red marble cat. Châteaubriand wrote: "I love in the cat the supreme indifference and dignity with which it can carry itself from salons to gutters. . . ."

It is difficult to explain how the Church revised its convictions on cats over the centuries beyond the magnanimity of Leone XII, but it should be remembered that many years before, the famous French cardinal statesman Richelieu (1585–1642) was a great friend of cats. He always hosted cats at his table, and after his death he left a great sum of money so that his numerous felines would be well taken care of even without his protection.

Other notable French cat-lovers of the nineteenth century included: Alexandre Dumas, fils, owner of a small private zoo, who was proclaimed "defense lawyer of cats of all the world"; George Sand, who had breakfast from the same cup as her cat; and Victor Hugo, who fashioned an armchair in the form of a throne for his cat.

The tradition of writing affectionately about cats has been preserved in France in our time thanks particularly to poet Jean Cocteau and Colette, a popular writer who had her photo-portrait taken in a feline pose as a sphinx.

English literature dedicated many pages to the behavior of the cat in society. Shakespeare spoke of cats with affection in "The Merchant of

Venice" and "Henry V." Rudyard Kipling, Nobel-Prize winner for literature, dedicated unforgettable pages to the cat.

Even a quick list of literary cat-lovers might never end. It is enough to enter the names Montaigne, Mérimée, Sardou, Eliot, Hemingway. One shouldn't forget the Nobel-Prize-winner Albert Schweitzer, who, after a tiring day among the lepers of Lambarene, relaxed by playing the organ and attending to the cats at the hospital.

Musical variations on the cat

Many famous musicians were inspired by the charm of cats. Domenico Scarlatti composed the "Fuga del Gatta" in the 1700s, in which he seemed touched by a cat that passed with incredible grace over the keyboard of the harpsichord.

Gioacchino Antonio Rossini (1792–1868) in his later years composed the "Duetto Buffo dei due Gatti," using two female voices that answer each other spiritually with the word "meow" in many variations. Maurice Ravel also wrote a realistic duet between cats in his short lyrical fantasy "L'enfant et les Sortile'ges." Other cats were impersonated in ballets; and the pas de deux in the "Sleeping Beauty" of Tchaikovsky should be remembered.

Edvard Grieg and Jules Massenet were also sincere lovers of cats. The list is very long. Remember that one side of the psychology of the cat is its sensitivity to music, so much so that an author defined it as "melomane." Our feline's passion for music is probably due to the fact that certain sounds produce a pleasurable sensation that reminds them of the love call of their partner. Everyone has seen a cat sleeping peacefully next to a record player, without being particularly interested in the voice of Frank Sinatra or the violin of Nathan Milstein.

Immortalized by great painters

Cats have inspired painters and sculptors to depict their images in the world of figurative art beginning with the feline head that represented the famous Egyptian goddess Bast. Numerous talismans and statuettes symbolizing the sacred cat remained intact from the Egyptian world after 4,000 years.

Important images, however, from the Greek and Roman classical periods are missing, if we exclude a few mosaics and frescoes from the Pompeian period. This void is explained by the Greek and Roman belief that the cat was a hunter of mice, a domestic embodiment of the lowest level and not a sacred animal capable of inspiring noble, artistic ideas.

The cat image often appears in ancient, heraldic art. The Romans incised cat forms on the flags of their legions. Many families that had names such as Katzen, Gatti, Gatteschi, Lechat, and Duchat had a cat sculpted on their shields. Goldsmiths also dedicated their attention to engraving the precious and elegant silhouette of the cat.

In paintings and sculpture, the cat was used as a model only after the Middle Ages when the punitive raids had ended. Leonardo da Vinci (1452–1519) painted the "Virgin of the Cat"; Albrecht Dürer depicted a cat that licked the feet of Eve; Jean Antoine Watteau immortalized the cat in his painting "The Sick Cat." Not even Veronese, Rubens, Bosch, Brueghel the Elder, Rembrandt, or Tintoretto were able to escape a fascination with the cat, nor did modern painters such as Delacroix, Renoir, Courbet, Gauguin, or Picasso. Particularly Edouard Manet, who loved to paint cats, used to observe them on the street from a distant window in his house.

The French writer Colette at her work table with her faithful cat next to her.

The French designer and commercial artist Alexandre Steinlen loved the suburbs and cats, which he hosted to the point where his house became known as "the cats' corner," because he gave shelter to many stray cats. Cats, of course, became famous from the posters of Steinlen who, publicizing milk and tea, was the first to immortalize cats in realistic animation.

Success in films
Manipulated and characterized in the way of the old fablers, the cat's personage was taken advantage of by the cinema with animated cartoons which became popular all over the world, such as Tom and Jerry, Krazy Kat, Sylvester the Cat, Felix, and the Pink Panther, who is without doubt a charming cat.

But in addition to cats drawn by Walt Disney studios or impersonated by people in costume (the musical *Cats*), there existed authentic cats that actually became stars of films and television. An exceptional case was Rhubarb, who was a born actor and loved to perform before the cameras, pirouetting until the late age of sixteen as if he were a kitten enjoying a large group of admirers. His real name was Orangey and he co-starred with Ray Milland in the film *Rhubarb*. Orangey went on to star in the TV series "Our Miss Brooks" where, as Minerva, he shared the spotlight with Eve Arden. Orangey also played Cat in the film *Breakfast at Tiffany's*. He was the prototype of television's Morris the Cat.

Television has contributed substantially to the popularity of cats since it renders them more dear, and increases the curiosity and concern of the people who fear their enigmatic glances.

In recent times technical perfections of photographic art have enabled the cat to be used in commercial publicity. Cats and kittens are very photogenic and can easily be used to advertise any product: greeting cards, candy boxes, calendars, toys, and food. It seems that we live in a time of some glory for the cat.

The proverbs of every country

Poets, novelists, and philosophers have left some thoughts about cats in their works and diaries, some of which is worth mentioning. In the nineteenth century the French historian Hippolyte Taine wrote this lapidary judgment: "I've met many thinkers and many cats, but the wisdom of cats is infinitely superior."

The French romantic poet Theophile Gautier said: "The pashas love tigers, I love cats, which are the tigers of the poor." And he also wrote: "God has created the cat to give man the pleasure of caressing the tiger." Jean Cocteau affirmed his preference for cats over dogs "because police cats don't exist."

Sayings, inspired by the assets and liabilities of cats, are numerous. They have identifiable qualities such as: sharp like a cat, false like a cat, to steal like a cat, agile like a cat, silent like a cat, sensual like a cat, to see in the dark like a cat, and be free like a cat.

The following are some cat proverbs familiar around the world:

Curiosity killed the cat.

While the cat's away, the mice will play.

There's more than one way to skin a cat.

The frenetic cat gives birth to blind cats. (Things done too quickly come out badly.)

The cat who often goes to the bacon will leave its paw there. (He who involves himself in illicit affairs is eventually discovered.)

He born of a cat, begets mice. (Certain dishonest tendencies are inherited.)

The cat who closed his eyes not to see the mice (one who doesn't concern himself in necessary and important things).

Dead cat (a person apparently meek, but who in reality hides another character).

Cat in a den (possessing an unconvincing quality).

Fight like cats and dogs.

There were four cats (a theater with few people).

To fall on one's feet like a cat (come out of a difficulty without damage).

Take a chestnut from the fire with the paw of a cat (a person who takes risks at the expense of others).

Cat music (devilish and out-of-tune music).

A perfect living machine

One point that may be stated without fear of disapproval is that the cat, whether of a great breed or from the street, is a beautiful animal created by nature. The cat is one of the most common house pets today, and it may be said that its popularity almost equals that of the dog. Its flexible body and elegant muscles compose a perfect "living machine" that complements itself with a vivacious intelligence, which renders it mysterious, clever, swift, unstoppable, brave, and whimsical.

This machine, however, only functions when it is in the right mood. A cat's day is not always active. After a few joyous outbursts, running up a tree, hunting some small animal, playing various games, and cleaning its body, it passes a good deal of time in meditative repose. It's an active hunter and game-player but not a walker. It tires more quickly than man and its energy level drops quite quickly. While a dog can run

Various interpretations of the cat: Michelangelo (top left); Picasso (top right); Giuseppe Maria Crespi (1665–1747) (center left); Jacob Jordaens (1593–1678) (center right); Tintoretto (bottom).

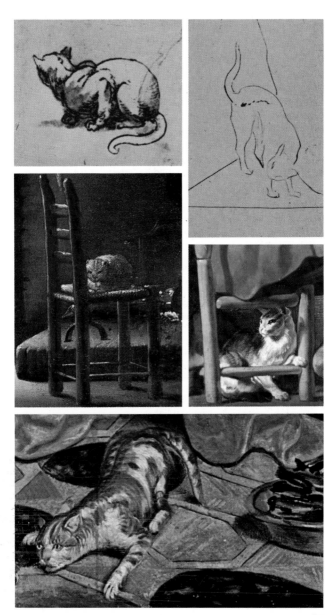

all day, the cat, after a short walk, is already dreaming of stretching out like a pasha on a warm rock or a soft cushion.

A full-grown cat is approximately 20 in. (50 cm.) in length. Add 10 or 12 in. (25 or 30 cm.) more for the tail. The medium weight of a male is 7 to 9 lb. (3.2 to 4 kg.) or more if well fed or of a breed that is larger, such as the Maine Coon or the British Shorthair; females are smaller.

There is record of a male cat that reached a weight of 42 lb. (19.5 kg.), but it was obviously a case of gigantism worthy of appearing in the *Guinness Book of World Records*.

The cat's claws and teeth are its weapons of offense and defense. Its claws are especially deadly; they come out of their sheath on command as soon as there's danger. Let us now turn to the particulars of the feline anatomy.

The cat has 245 bones, quite fragile, of which about twenty are in its tail. The vertebral column is formed by fifty-one vertebrae; its round head has its cranium protected in front. There are twenty-six ribs in its chest. The forehead is short and curved; its jaws are arched. The pelvis, long and straight, is so well-balanced and light that when it falls from a great height, it lands on its feet 90 percent of the time. High falls could be fatal because the weight of its body would increase from the acceleration of the fall. Its body, turning in the fall, would lose its rhythm and upon landing would most likely fracture its limbs. The cat's equilibrium is an atavistic inheritance, which developed when it passed the better part of the day in trees, jumping from branches and climbing tree trunks.

Even now the cat easily climbs trees, but has difficulty getting down because it is determined to do it with its head down to see its path. It often happens that, aroused by curiosity, cats get themselves in trouble on tree branches or on rooftops.

Thanks to its equilibrium, the cat, unlike the dog, doesn't suffer from car- or sea-sickness, although most cats do not particularly care for journeys and don't enjoy watching new and interesting landscapes from a window.

Its paws are a little short in proportion to its long body, which gives it a certain elegance. An exemplary, long paw would certainly not be very pleasing. Its limbs touch the earth with its toes. The anterior paws hold five nails; the posterior paws hold four.

The cat's tail is always quite long (except in the manx) and plays a large role in its beauty. The female usually is not a very large animal but grows to a pleasantly thin size. She may have six or eight teats, which are subdivided into those of the chest, abdomen, and groin; they are individual entities like little bumps concealed in the skin, noticeable only when they are swollen from pregnancy.

Four canines for fighting

The cat has thirty teeth (dogs have forty-two), sixteen of which are located in the upper jaw and fourteen in the lower. The most important ones for battle, defense, and eating are the four daggerlike canines, slightly inclined inward (making it impossible for its prey to escape), immediately visible when the cat opens its mouth to yawn, as are the fourteen molars. The small incisors that complete the denture serve little purpose.

Kittens teethe a couple of weeks after birth. Soon the mother stops feeding her kittens when their teeth cause pain to her teats. These so-called milk teeth are substituted by permanent ones when the kitten is about seven or eight months old. The cat doesn't chew or grind food

The teeth of a cat. In the box, from the left: the molars (shown in the rectangle); the premolars (box); the canines (triangle); the incisors (center box).

but swallows it in pieces, which are then broken down by active gastric acids.

The cat's tongue is like a small rasp, which can be felt in a moment of affection when it licks your hand. This tongue is made up of minute, cornified papillae, which are retroverted backwards to allow the animal to "grate" its coat to make it shiny and clean. The roughness also causes the wounds of its prey to bleed more.

The pear-shaped stomach can hold approximately three-quarters of a pint in liquid and food. It is a small amount, but in this limited space it can concentrate many calories, obtained primarily from the digestion of meat and fish. Consequently, the intestine is only seven feet (twenty-six feet in man), so that digestion is always a bit difficult. Proportionately, the liver is larger, divided into five lobes.

The cat's pulse doesn't exceed thirty beats per minute and is quiet and imperceptible. When the whisper of difficult breathing is heard, it is a sign of some irregularity.

Its beautiful fur

The coat and skin of the cat play a very important role in protecting the maintenance of its corporal equilibrium. They form an efficient barrier to the external world, preventing an excessive loss of water and defending the animal from physical harm from heat, cold, strong sun rays, and germs.

The looseness of the skin enables the better part of any possible wound to be superficial. The skin is only one millimeter thick on its stomach and a maximum of four millimeters on its neck.

The thick winter coat and the lighter summer one regulate the body

temperature during the change of seasons. The skin's shine is due to sebum, a lubricant secreted by the sebaceous glands of the skin. The sebum, which forms a film on the skin, is rich in vitamin D: by licking itself, the cat consumes a small quantity that it uses as a protection for the organism.

The cat's fur is the most spectacular and important component of its body. It is the essential element for the animal's beauty and elegance. The fur may be short, long, hard, soft, silky, coarse, thick, or wavy, but always offers an essential motive of aesthetic judgment. Cultivators of curious statistics state that up to 200 hairs for every square millimeter can be found on a cat's body. When a cat's skin is very dry, its coat can emit static electricity, which can be felt when we caress a cat's hair.

The various numbers and varieties of breeds not only have different textures of fur but also disparate colorations. The most common colors are gray-blue, black, red, white, brown, and many shades and combinations such as lilac, blue, cream, smoke, silver, chocolate, etc.

Why the cat sees in the dark

A cat's sight is said to be its most extraordinary sense. Each eye can encompass a range of vision of 287°, which enhanced by the mobility of the head can explore a vast horizon and always be ready to defend itself. It probably cannot focus on close objects very well, but beyond seven feet nothing escapes its view.

In daylight its vision is perfect. Also at night, when assisted by a distant streetlight or a ray of moonlight, it can see quite clearly. For this reason, the iris (the disc-shaped membrane with a hole in the center that separates the two parts of the eye) can dilate the pupil (the circular

(left) At night the pupil dilates so that the cat can see in the dark.
(right) In daylight the cat's pupil closes.

aperture situated in the center of the iris), and the smallest bit of nocturnal light is magnified forty to fifty times in the eye.

Such light amplification is due to an internal cellular lining, called *tapetum lucidum*, of a yellowish color, which acts like a sort of bright mirror, reflecting the light on the retina (the very delicate membrane which receives the lighted impressions).

Even though the cat can see in the dark, its pupils cannot take in the sun's direct rays. The cat defends itself against them by modifying the opening of the pupil, which may be reduced to a barely visible vertical crack, cutting out the desired amount of light. It is a phenomenon that every cat-owner knows well.

The eyes of various breeds often have beautiful and mysterious hues (gray, light blue, green, gold), and it is possible to find a cat with different colored eyes. Each eye possesses a nictating membrane, which acts like an additional eyelid closing horizontally.

If we are to believe that which some experimentors have said, certain well-trained cats can distinguish red and blue from other colors, but red appears light green to them and they confuse white and yellow. In other words, the cat may suffer from color blindness.

Just like many other mammals, when the kittens are born they're blind. Since their retina isn't completely developed, they begin to distinguish something of the world that awaits them after a few days. Mature vision is achieved after the first three months. From that moment on, this sense is extremely essential as a matter of life or death. Cats who lose their vision, either by accident or during a fight, do not live long, especially if they live in the streets where they are easy targets of collision or aggression.

Les Chats, *Lithograph by Edouard Manet, 1868.*

Excellent hearing

The cat's hearing is sensitive and receptive to the level of sonar vibrations of a frequency beyond the maximum perceptible by the human ear.

The cat is able to pick up from a distance the rustle of a mouse and even isolate it from the midst of other noises that could confuse it. Its outer ear is erect like an antenna ready to capture sounds and send them into a well-developed eardrum case. It can thus be affirmed that the cat has an acute and selective capacity for localizing a sound and be off only by a few inches to a yard. The cat uses hearing for its own pleasure. If it is attracted by an interesting noise, it prefers not to pay attention to its owner's call. With respect to the submission of a dog, the cat obeys its instincts first and serves its own needs and desires first.

If such a perceptive ear could be put to useful purposes, we would have a better guard than an electronic theft alarm; if we could also succeed in making the cat's claws come out in the presence of intruders, there wouldn't be a house or factory without cats. This would then probably cause the end of the dynasty of guard dogs.

Some cats tend to become deaf in old age, but compensate for the handicap by making their sight and sense of smell more acute and becoming more sensitive to vibrations. Many cats with a white coat and light blue eyes remain completely deaf from birth.

The outer ear is furnished with a small barrier of skin that impedes small particles from penetrating the inside. At the same time, dust and wax may form annoying deposits in the delicate, sensitive hearing channel. To avoid having the cat hurt itself by trying to scratch the itch with its nails, it is necessary to clean the inner ear with a cotton ball moistened with vaseline, or with a Q-tip, always avoiding deep penetration.

The tomcat does not willingly accept this kind of intervention, but if the owner habituates the cat to this from birth, he shouldn't run into any difficulty afterwards.

The pleasures of the sense of smell

As with its wild ancestors, the cat's sense of smell has also been developed. No odor escapes the cat, so it isn't necessary for the cat to see its food to decide whether to eat it; it is enough to smell it. The dog immediately swallows a mouthful of whatever is brought to it, but the cat inspects it with its nose, even with suspicion.

Appetizing meats are not sensed by taste but by smell. Every type of meat (beef, pork, lamb) and every kind of it (liver, lung, various entrails) has a different odor. Cats possess very delicate palates, demonstrating a fine scale of preferences.

Their sense of smell is so unique and particular that the perfume of certain plants can arouse an intense interest in them. That is true of catnip (Nepeta cataria), which grows in the temperate zones of Europe and North America, but can be cultivated in a garden or in a pot on a terrace. Cats like the particular perfume of this plant very much, and it has been chemically isolated; this scent is used on toys for cats.

Not all cats are sensitive to this odor, but those which are enter into a strange state of intense pleasure after having smelled it. It is believed that this plant essence has a druglike effect, because certain cats remain immobile, staring into space. The same type of behavior has been verified in the wild felines, such as the lion, leopard, and puma, when they come in contact with the catnip.

The cat is also attracted to the scent of the people who are dear to it. Affectionate house cats very often sleep on a coat or sweater, not only for its softness but for its owner's scent.

Certain viruses may cause the cat to lose its sense of smell temporarily. If this occurs the animal often loses its appetite for normal foods and becomes attracted to particular delicacies such as liver and herring, which emanate a strong odor. Loss of this sense can also cause modification of the cat's sexual behavior, affecting its ability to distinguish males from females, and to identify a castrated cat, which would be rejected as a good companion.

The sense of taste is changeable

The sense of taste is as developed as the sense of smell. The tongue's taste buds prefer salty and sour tastes, more than sweetness and bitterness. But this is disputable, because many cats love to eat cookies. Cats can quickly recognize flavors: a one-day-old kitten can distinguish a salty liquid from a bland one. But as the years pass the acuteness of this sense diminishes, as happens also to man and other animals.

The cat therefore remains a difficult guest with its tastes and appetites. It gets tired of the same food and will look for something else by jumping on the kitchen table. To change its diet, the cat will go about stealing in the house or search outside or kill little animals (the game is coupled with a reward of food). However, many cats become addicted to one brand of cat food or type of food and stubbornly insist on nothing else.

When it is ill, the cat unhappily accepts medicinals, but often prefers to search for itself in the garden, field, or forest for the correct herbs that it instinctively knows to be necessary to cure itself. Often acting as its own veterinarian, the cat proves to be right.

The whiskers as radar

The whiskers are the most sensitive of the sensory organs. They are situated in the skin above the lips and sense the slightest touch or pressure. In the dark of the night, when not even the eyes can find a ray of light, in a room or outside, the whiskers assume the function of radar that perceives the presence and nature of a nearby object. They also protect the cat's sight from every potentially dangerous object (a thornbush, wall, trap) that touches the whiskers first, so that the cat closes its eyes immediately.

The whiskers also sense air currents caused by moving objects, so that the cat "feels" even without having to touch an object. The loss of whiskers or their elimination by scissors would obstruct the cat's ability to freely move about.

Paws to know the world

In addition to jumping, running, and moving about, the paws also are important for feeling and are used to investigate suspicious objects. A puppy, curious to know the world, smells everything that comes its way. But the cat, more than any other animal, is full of trepidations. It first puts a paw toward the new thing, touches it timidly, then proceeds more decisively, and only after that, smells it.

The cushions on the flat of the foot transmit information to the cat by picking up any vibration. More than for an innate sense of personal hygiene does the cat maintain a clean body. To conserve maximum efficiency for its complex sensory organs, a clean body, from its coat to its extremities, is vital.

The cat is particularly complicated and finicky in terms of its taste and appetite.

Resistance to pain

Considered to be the animal of nine lives, the cat tries not to show its suffering, even if a pain is real. Such gifts of resistance permit the cat to overcome certain minor pathological manifestations and to enjoy a benign evolution. Excluding the muzzle, which is vulnerable, the cat is relatively insensitive to high temperatures. Even though the cat is capable of resisting heat and pain, it is not an animal that will voluntarily put itself through an uncomfortable situation.

The reaction to pain varies from cat to cat: some become aggressive if a wound is touched or if a syringe is used on it for an injection; others, however, react with complete faith and tend to purr, intuitively knowing that the human hand is working for its benefit.

A frequently discussed psychology

The cat's psychology is open to vast and unending discussion. It remains a profound mystery, because in addition to the typical qualities of felines (independence, curiosity, interest in hunting, jealousy, and sleep) there is also an unclassifiable and enigmatic aspect to the cat's psyche.

Every cat has its own secret and deceptive personality that can break down any theory. There are cats whose psyches are characterized as timid, impudent, obedient, stubborn, tranquil, spiteful, courageous, vile, or nervous with all of the above with every possible nuance.

Dominant traits in the cat are individualism and a well-defined and varied personal character, which psychologically renders all of them, (even those of the same breed and litter) different.

Cats use their nails or claws to defend themselves and to climb. At other times the claws withdraw into their skin pockets. The small cushioned area at the bottom of the paw can sense the slightest vibration.

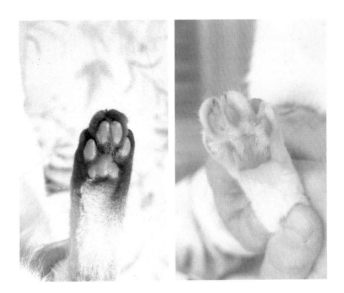

For every breed, however, we can outline in general terms a psychological portrait quite stable and believable. But this standard can be disproven from one generation to the next. In the psychological labyrinth of the cat, one must step with caution, even if one is aware of the norm and the exceptions.

The cat has an ample and very advanced cerebral hemisphere, typical of intelligent creatures. The physical growth of a kitten's brain develops quickly and is more or less complete at five months old. The normal growth of the brain also depends on the amount of sensory stimuli the kitten experiences, which is by the mother and humans. A solitary life and sparse nutrition, on the other hand, can irremediably damage the brain's development.

The wonderful egotist
A social hierarchy doesn't exist among cats. A loose order develops between males, especially during mating season. Every cat is a solitary individual in the world. Its ancestors never lived in groups or in packs like dogs, but each one managed alone. One other peculiarity should be noted: if a certain number of cats are by necessity forced to live together, they will develop a more fraternal relationship than dogs. This is perhaps explainable by the fact that they nurture a social life, even if this behavior could be catalogued among the many personality nuances of the species.

Rather than assist humans in hunting, the cat egotistically hunted on its own and refused to cooperate with training schools that gave degrees to the horse and dog.

The various animals considered domestic (dog, horse, swine) by nature have a tendency to gather in packs and always elect a leader. The cat, on the other hand, living isolated and with the idea of the world free of bondage, doesn't recognize the quality of commander in other cats or in humans.

Cats can easily adapt to a change in circumstances because they remember what they learn and then adapt their experiences to various new situations as they present themselves. For example, the capacity to hunt occurs only if the mother is a good hunter. She teaches her young (who will always remember) various hunting techniques, which produces good poachers. The young of an inactive mother may not learn to kill or to play with little animals.

Actually, the cat's behavior is sometimes difficult to understand. It is capable of seeing everything with sleepy eyes, and can suddenly spot a mouse, or it may remain indifferent to its owner's call but then suddenly respond to a bowl that reminds it of the availability of food.

The cat is a marvelous egotist that's not interested in great things, but rather pays attention to those things that are related to its own interests. The cat always likes a human presence, especially when the person loves it. The cat will seek out a caress and express its satisfaction with its famous purr only when it has the need. If it returns home after a few days absence, it is capable of receiving you with coldness, but as soon as it strikes its fancy, it is ready for your hand.

Learns without servility

The cat is an animal full of pride and decorum that rarely and patronizingly accepts being taught or imposed upon. In order not to learn something or to work, the cat would suffer hunger and inclement weather, and resort to theft and sleeping inside an abandoned box in a gutter.

Only from an expert, patient hand could a cat learn something like opening a door, giving a paw, sitting in front of a bowl of food, playing dead, rolling on the floor at command, or going to fetch an object.

A cat will allow itself to be somewhat mastered if it foresees some advantage to itself. It will learn a game only because its success corresponds to a delicacy or the insistence of a dominant personality. The best age for this training is when the cat is four to five months old. When it is mature, it will refuse to obey because it will perceive these entertainments as nonsense.

Sometimes cats also learn something on their own initiative (knocking on windows to get in, grabbing doorknobs to get out, hiding food in boxes, opening refrigerators to eat a delicious fish).

Up until the age of five to six months a cat plays, jumps, has fun, discovers life, but does this as an unordered and unconscious activity. It will successfully effect movements and outbursts out of a precise necessity and only when it is the one to decide. Sometimes, however, it will give in to the owner's desires, but only in small ways and in a climate of affection, linked to a pleasure of its own.

Inconsistency is its occupation

For several hours a day, the cat sleeps, or pretends to sleep. But it is enough that a creak or small suspicious noise intervenes that the cat suddenly wakes up with open eyes and pointing ears.

In its everyday life, the cat is inconsistent. For brief periods it may sleep on a certain cushion or in a particular corner, or for weeks it may

The cat: sly, solitary. A magnificent egotist.

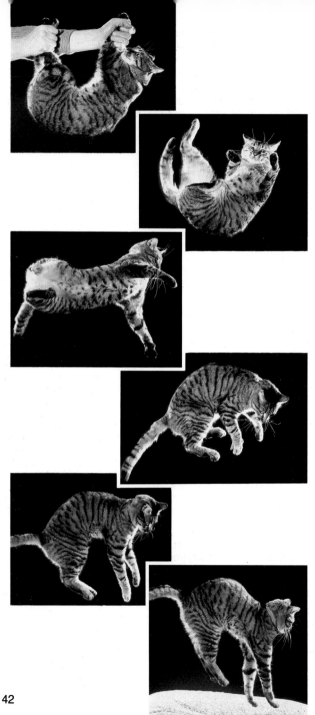

eat a meal of commercial cat food. Then suddenly it may change its mind and look for other places to sleep and refuse its regular food. However, it is consistent in its affection for the people in the house and kept indoors, always uses its litter box, fortunately. If it were not such a clean animal, it would certainly be less well received. It would not have been welcome in apartments, and perhaps today it would still be leading a stray life or be behind the bars of a zoo, or be like other feline species that walk the path of extinction.

Change, memory, curiosity

In its psyche flourishes a resistance to any changes in family, territory, or habit. If another cat enters in a house that has been its domain, often an old cat will pretend to hunt the young intruder, or it will ignore it with great style, showing no interest.

The cat has an innate sense of curiosity. It is aware of a little ball in motion, strange objects, or the contents of an open drawer. Notwithstanding its apparent fragility and delicate beauty, it is strange and bold. But it will tend to ignore things larger than itself, including dogs, but against which it knows how to defend itself. It has been surmised that when the cat enlarges itself in front of an enemy, it intends to appear bigger and to strike by instilling fear. Is it prudent or cowardly? We who love cats say that it is a matter of wisdom.

A timid and fearful cat that flees the callings and presence of man has certainly experienced some mistreatment that has made it suspicious; it is up to us to rekindle its faith by putting a plate of food in front of it and speaking from a distance with soothing tones. Almost all cats will not remain indifferent to that well-noted call that we emit from our lips that has the affectionate sound of a kiss thrown through the air.

The memory of a cat is not short: it will be able, often for some time, to recognize not only who treats it well but also who mistreats it. Cats have a considerable sense of orientation, connected in a certain way to affection and fidelity. Many felines have confronted long distances, overcoming difficult natural obstacles, in order to touch again upon familiar land. And it has been deduced, like certain evolved migrant birds, that cats can cross unknown areas by using the sun's shadow and the magnetic field. When they are close to home, there are no problems because they recognize the place by noises and odors.

The defense of territory

The cat has not forgotten the distant past when, living in total freedom, it had to defend its own territory from invasion by other animals, enemies, or friends. Its concept of private property still lives on today.

According to those learned in animal psychology, the territory of the cat can be imagined as divided into three concentric zones. In the center is its own, inviolable refuge that coincides with its habitation or its surroundings and is represented by the place where the animal sleeps. The second zone is the area in which it walks, also forbidden to intruders. The third zone is constituted by the vast external area of the hunt. The male divides its territory by the garden, the field, and the forest in which it feels master, marking it with urine and feces. In this way it intends to hold at bay any other cats that dare to enter its own territory.

Intelligent, inconsistent, prone to sudden changes in temperament, jealous, curious. The cat, an asocial and autosufficient animal, is not easily mastered, and is never servile.

However, among cats that know one another there is a kind of compromise for which the supremacy of borders can be worked out and getting along occurs without difficulty. But they defend their space against any intrusion by other animals to the degree that they will run home rather than share, bringing out again their innate stubborn sense of independence and absolutism.

The problem is very much lessened for spayed cats whose urine has lost its characteristic odor, and also for those well taken care of, fed on schedule, fondled, and already in possession of a defended and untouchable corner where it sleeps undisturbed.

The kitten is born with the instinct not to dirty its own refuge. It hates filth, and for this reason, it learns very quickly to use the proverbial litter box. The instinctive preoccupation not to be discovered by an enemy compels it to bury its bodily waste.

In the event that a cat begins to dirty other areas, ignoring the teachings of the forest, it must be taught to do otherwise immediately, because once an adult it will be difficult to change its habits. The cat should promptly be placed in a box, which should then be cleaned regularly and periodically sterilized. The above doesn't apply to cats who frequent gardens.

No cat, castrated or whole, purebred or random-bred, can renounce its passion for wandering either briefly or at length, being devoted to an interest in the hunt, adventure, or sex. It possesses a decisive sense of orientation, which enables it to know how to find its way home. The attachment to its home, owner, and the certainty of finding food, lead it back home even after a few days absence.

Extremely curious, kittens prefer to learn about the world on their own.

The cat does not tolerate competition within its own territory.

No cat-owner could ever say that it is complete master over his or her cat.

The barometric sensibility

Many animals like the dog, horse, donkey, and evolved birds like swallows are sensitive to the weather and show signs of nervousness and depression when a storm is approaching. It is known that dogs, horses, and other wild animals can sense an approaching earthquake. Particular howls, kicking in stables, and unexpected flights of wolves and squirrels have given warning on many occasions of an approaching tragedy.

The cat also has a barometric sensitivity: before a rainfall, even without evident manifestations, it will appear agitated and seek shelter. It isn't accurate to say that the cat can forewarn us of the coming of a storm because it is gifted with a magic sensitivity. It can perceive a decrease in atmospheric pressure, minor earth tremors, the smell of distant rain, or other changes in a daily routine such as when its owners are about to leave the house. All of this may be defined as a sixth sense, but nothing of what the cat "feels" with respect to the atmosphere has any scientific base. There is a popular notion that states when a cat licks its paw or puts it in its ear, it is a sign of rain or a change in atmosphere. Farmers of the last century observed the behavior of cats during droughts while waiting for rain.

The cat has an instinctive dislike for water, either in the form of rain, puddles, frost on the grass, damp earth, or a bath at home. When there are threatening clouds, the cat hides. The cat is not well protected against water because its coat does not have a layer of protective fat. Its fur insulates it from the cold but cannot adapt to water. The cat does not have a "raincoat," as do certain breeds of dog such as the Labrador Retriever, which spends a lot of time in the water. In addition, the cat doesn't know how to shake off excess water and free itself from humidity when trying to dry itself.

If pushed by dramatic necessity, however, as when sought by a pack of dogs or when defending its young from danger, cats know how to handle a river's current or the dangers of a lake. In particular situations of pressing hunger, the cat can even prove itself to be a good swimmer and fisherman.

The ancient instinct of the hunt

The house cat, which is usually well nourished by its owner with particular food or leftovers from the table, logically does not have the need to go hunting. Even the lion with a full stomach will stretch out in the shade of a tree. However, the cat continues to believe that it is a carnivorous predator just as man arms himself with a rifle on Sunday to repeat the hunting ritual of his ancestors.

As stated previously, the best hunting techniques were taught by the mother, who brought small, living animals such as mice to kill as if it were a game. By playing with their teeth and claws, the kittens learned to apply this to hunting prey for food. To kill a mouse or a bird remains an elicited instinct for the house cat, which doesn't subside with the passage of years. This fact is regretted by the owner whenever his or her cat brings home a small mouse or bird.

The cat places itself patiently still for hours in front of an opening, in wait for the desired quest to come out, trying to place itself in the correct spot so as not to be discovered. It then takes an astonishingly agile and precise leap, falling in a way that the back paws touch the ground and the front ones seize the prey.

The tongue, covered with small, hooked, cornified papillae, serves to maintain a clean and shiny coat.

Prey capture begins with a stalking gait.

The passage from the game to premeditated killing is very quick. The sentence is decreed by hunger. Certain stray and semi-stray cats kill small, wild animals (mice, rabbits, birds) by a bite at the base of the neck, which breaks the spinal cord, causing instant death. The cat finds the exact spot to bite by the sensitive spots at the base of their teeth.

Observation in factories and courtyards reveals that cats are not infallible killers because 80 percent of birds and 50 percent of mice manage to escape from their attack.

Cats are praised for killing a mouse but blamed for catching a bird; the truth is that for the cat to hunt one or the other makes no difference. Some people put a bell on the cat's collar in order to warn unsuspecting birds of the approaching danger. The problem is that mice also learn to hide as soon as they hear the ringing of the bell.

He who owns a cat knows that sometimes a fish or piece of meat, which is on the kitchen table, ends up in the mouth of the cat. Even though reprimanded, as soon as the desire hits, the cat will repeat the theft, even if its own plate is full.

It becomes evident that the cat is not as domesticated as the dog; its heart has remained partly in the wild and it still hasn't concluded a totally civil pact with man. It does prove itself to be a friend by showing a bit of authentic affection, of interest and whim.

Even though cats are generally solitary and egotistical hunters, they sometimes carry the spoils of their prey home to share with their fellow cats or as a gift to the owner. It is an affectionate demonstration accepted with a certain degree of horror, especially when it's a matter of toads and mice. This is the social, almost altruistic, side of the cat.

The cat seizing its prey.

A varied language

Although individualists, cats have one point in common: the language with which they can express many feelings and can make themselves understood by man. It is an extremely varied idiom that is based on two diverse sonar emissions: the meow and the purr. The first is translated into sounds of many modulations, each with its own significance; the second can be defined as a kind of interior language, which vibrates from a closed mouth.

In communicating among themselves, cats are very adept. They recognize each other by odors and if they've already become friends, they greet each other by rubbing noses as lap dogs do, or they smell each others' head and anal region. The glandular secretions of these areas identify each cat by a particular odor. If they truly get along, the cats rub against each other, marking the coat of the other with an odor for the next meeting. Cats rub up against their owners for the same reason.

Cats do not possess a vast vocabulary, and only after the first twelve weeks of life do they begin to reproduce adult sounds. The writer Theodore Hoffmann, one of the most representative figures of German romanticism and author of the story "The Cat Murr," said that the cat "has the incredible gift of expressing the one word 'meow' in many ways— joy, pain, delight, abduction, fear, desperation, in sum, all the sensations and passions." The most intense vocal language is expressed in mating.

Often many aspects of the feline language are repeated to establish relationships with people and other animals; that is, the same behavior that cats use among themselves are also used with dogs and owners. Cats born and raised in a house develop an individual character that they put into action only for use with their owners. It shows that felines can modify their behavior according to their present environment. When it enjoys the esteem of its owners in a serene atmosphere, the cat relates its actual feelings; it reveals itself and opens up to sincerity.

The cat expresses itself with a meow, but within this sound are enclosed many feelings: appetite, love, unrest, joy, anger, and pain calibrated according to the cat's present state of mind using tones either soft, dramatic, calm, or insistent. Some breeds, like the Siamese, are more vocal than others.

The cat's vocabulary is greater than the dog's. When meeting one of its own kind, the feline can emit more than fifty different sounds, which vary in tone from harsh to acute. The cat forms "words" that assume a precise meaning for other cats. And if in the future it will be possible to translate the phrases that comprise the cat's language, what kind of judgment would the cat give to man?

The cat possesses a sweet sound, the purr, which it uses to express joy, momentary well-being, and affection for its owner. It is a musical sound repeated at length when the cat is happy. This particular vibration, considered "ron-ron," is produced by the rubbing of vocal cords and is a typical characteristic of felines. The tiger, with even greater authority, abandons itself to this musical finesse.

The cat's body language is expressed with more than sixty gestures, such as the tilt of the head, the position of the tail and ears, and facial expressions. The most obvious ones are the puffing out of its body to make itself bigger in front of the enemy, the arching of its back to give it a monstrous aspect, and the rubbing up against the legs of its owner to obtain food or caresses.

When the cat purrs or sways its tail, it is expressing some inner need or desire. It doesn't know how to hide anything, neither love nor contrariness.

Unlike the dog, when the cat's tail moves slowly, it is nervous and prefers not to be disturbed. A sign of contentment, however, is shown when it stretches its tail straight out (coupled with purring), and this almost always happens when it realizes that food is being prepared for it.

When, however, the cat relaxes its tail or arches it with the hairs straight up, it is a sign of anger or fear of the presence of some adversary.

The affectionate female
The cat expresses affection for its owners by rubbing its muzzle and body against their legs, by licking a hand or face with its coarse tongue, or by lying with its stomach up awaiting a caress and then immediately biting the hand that touches it. It often closes its eyes from the pleasure of physical contact with a loved person.

Females are in general more disposed to affectionate manifestations than males. A nice ritual that precedes the amorous moment should be remembered: before sitting in the lap of its owner or before stretching out on a cushion that is particularly favored, the female (and sometimes the male) performs a curious maneuver similar to a pin dance. The cat pulls out its nails and sweetly pushes them into the fabric on which it desires to rest itself.

Sleep
Cats sleep two-thirds of the day, and it is not known why their sleep is twice as long as that of other animals. But the length of the daily sleep

Arched back and hair on end: the cat finds itself before the enemy.

is variable and seems conditioned by a well-satisfied appetite, sexual stimuli, age, and the seasons. Young and old cats sleep more than a healthy adult cat. The combination of warmth, security, and a full stomach can provoke drowsiness at every hour of the day for a cat of any age.

For cats that stay at home, the ideal place to sleep is an armchair, bed, or the owner's clothing in a laundry basket, or on a window sill. Stray cats are happy to nestle into straw or in an abandoned box.

The cat makes numerous movements with its paws and whiskers while sleeping, which give the impression that it is dreaming. Feline insomnia is unknown. The usual useless experiments have shown that when prohibited to sleep for a week, a cat dies. Humanity is cruel to have made these lab observations.

A glance at the breeds
He who desires to own a purebred cat should turn to a breeder, a cat association, or a specialized shop for cats. A breeder knows the identity of the parents of the kittens and can furnish the cat's pedigree. It would then be possible to approximate the future good qualities of the kitten that is about to be bought. The breeders of the great breeds—Persian/Longhair, Siamese, Abyssinian, Burmese, and so on—can be approached at cat shows that are organized at least once a year in major cities.

Preference for one cat over another is a question of personal taste. Before buying a cat it is wise for the potential owner to know something about the character of the breed being considered, and about the par-

ticular care that is needed (if the coat is combed or brushed, if the animal has a calm or unstable character, if it is of a robust constitution or is susceptible to disease).

There are more than forty cat breeds to choose from, and each has its own personality: adult Persian/Longhair cats are extremely placid, while Oriental breeds (particularly Siamese) are somewhat high-strung. Siamese require much affection, which they return. Rex cats are extroverts; the American Shorthair loves to play with children; the Chartreux is a tenacious hunter of mice; British and European Shorthairs are very sweet.

Among the breeds with long hair, Persians/Longhairs are the most difficult to care for. They need to be combed daily as do the Angoras and Balinese. In choosing a breed, it is important to be aware of the average temperature of the house, because a hot environment is not good for a Persian/Longhair, and a Siamese cannot be in a cold one. The American Shorthair can survive almost all climates.

When purchasing a cat, it is absolutely necessary to demand, aside from a pedigree, a vaccination certificate stating which shots have been given and when. A pedigreed cat should have a stabilized character with no hereditary defects. In reality there is good and bad in every breed and each cat should be judged individually.

If one is interested in acquiring a particular breed but doesn't want to spend too much, a type that differs slightly from the official standard because of some small defect, an imperfect color of the coat or eyes, may be bought. It will always be a beautiful house cat even if sold at a discount. These are referred to as cats of "pet quality."

When a cat is chosen, either pedigreed or without registration papers, it is important to examine the kitten and the place where it was bred. First impressions should be heeded. It is essential that kittens are born and raised in an environment that's warm, clean, and isolated because the cold and dirt are carriers of disease and too much noise could have disturbed its nervous system.

It is necessary to be sure that the kitten is happy and that its weight is in proportion to its age. Make sure that infections do not exist. Observation of the eyes, ears, nose, teeth, coat, abdomen, and anus is needed. Bad signs are running or smelly ears, bloated stomach, coughing, sneezing, lack of appetite, lack of energy, parasites in the coat, distorted paws, irregular breathing, and diarrhea. If a pedigreed kitten is purchased, one should know that its full coat and color may not develop until after a few months.

The price of a cat varies according to the breed, the beauty of its parents, quality of the pedigree, and the classifications and prizes obtained at shows by its ancestors. It is necessary to be cautious of a cat offered at a price too modest. A Show cat is at its maximum value at about one year for males, eighteen months for females.

Even if the acquisition is accompanied with all of the guarantees, a seasonal visit to a veterinarian is necessary. The wise owners of cats know that every animal should have its own veterinarian just as every member of a family should have its own doctor.

Male and female, pro and con
If reproduction is not intended or if there's the idea of sterilization in the future, it doesn't matter whether a male or female is purchased. They are equally intelligent, beautiful, and pleasant. Males grow a bit larger and may be a bit more aggressive, independent, and will have a tendency

to keep to themselves sometimes, but castration will alter much of this.

The female is more affectionate than the male by nature, easily purrs and, except for short mating periods, is more house-oriented.

The cat's sex is not very evident in the first weeks, so an untrained eye may confuse a male with a female. It is very easy to make this mistake with a litter of males and females together. The rule states that there is less space between the anal hole and the genitals in a female than there is in a male.

A male cat reaches sexual maturity between six and eight months old. If allowed to leave the house, it will begin to inspect the surroundings, to mark the territory with its urine, and to find a companion. Sometimes it will relieve itself on a door, and the odor of its urine is decidedly unpleasant.

Masters in twenty-four hours
The kitten taken from its mother will not immediately be able to nurture itself by licking a plate of broth or swallowing little pieces of cut-up meat. It will not break away too soon because, more than other carnivorous animals, the cat needs maternal milk, which is rich in protein, fat, vitamins and minerals, preventing disease and promoting growth.

The time to bring a kitten home is when it is two months old. It will feel at home in a new environment within twenty-four hours, forgetting its mother and siblings. If it were to meet them after some time, it wouldn't recognize them; they would be strange cats of whom it could become upset.

A cat of six months to a year, if it hasn't been shocked by difficult experiences, accustoms itself in a family where it doesn't lack food and

The Burmese combines affection and intelligence in an innate sense of reservedness. It has a loud voice.

Notwithstanding its apparent laziness, the Chartreux/British Blue is a tenacious hunter of mice. Meek, affectionate, and clever, it's an excellent friend for apartment living.

The Birman is a good and sociable cat, particularly adaptable to calm people, which it loves in silence with total devotion and fidelity. Even when playing, it is quiet and wise, without the impetuosity of the Siamese.

The Maine Coon is intelligent, clever, affectionate, and a home-lover, but at the same time it is a great hunter.

(top) If the cat's tail is wagging, it means that it is restless. It is best to leave it alone. (bottom) How the cat changes its expression before combat. From left to right, as aggression increases. From top to bottom, as fear increases. At bottom left, maximum aggression and maximum fear: the cat attacks because there is no way to escape.

affection. But be careful. Some female stray cats, shocked and mal-treated, transfer their fears of humans, other animals, and noise to their young. If one is in possession of a rambunctious kitten, it must be patiently taught the ways of living in a house, offered appetizing food, caressed only when it approaches spontaneously, careful that it doesn't scratch, and doesn't run for a door that is suddenly pushed open.

Learns its own name?
The cat is an instinctive animal, following actions which are held ego-tistically useful to itself. It will learn, however, its name rather quickly, especially if it is used with the call to dinner. But on other occasions, it will play possum or will go about its own business even though called repeatedly.

It should be given a short, sweet name of a couple of syllables so that the cat can remember it more easily. Someone gave his cat the name: "Doctor Livingston, I presume," and complained that his cat pre-tended to ignore his call.

A cat can be taught to answer to its name only if an affectionate and faithful relationship exists between the cat and its owner. The name must be repeated constantly during games, before and after meals, and when it has abandoned itself to some loving encounter.

First contact with living things
The hours in which a kitten is awake are completely occupied with playing, an influential activity in the development of dexterity, intelli-gence, and of other "arts," which make it become an adult sensitive to the good and bad situations of the future. It is precisely in the first months of life that the kitten undergoes the most important psychological and physical changes.

It is generally the mother who stimulates this development, but the behavior of the people in the family can also have a decisive effect. Stimuli influence the function of the brain; consequently young cats that have been correctly treated grow up less emotional and more curious, happy, disposed to learn new things, and sure of themselves. Orphan cats that have never even had contact with humans grow up timid or aggressive in rapports with their own kind and with society.

In the first four to five months, the kitten encounters and recognizes people, dogs, toys, small animals, cars, noises, good and bad food, good and bad manners, developing particular reactions to everything at an early age.

Kittens begin to play when they're about four weeks old, and their enjoyment becomes more elaborate as they grow. Playing keeps it happy and awake, brings out its hunting instinct, stimulates its reflexes, and is a necessity. Everything that moves attracts it. But rather than leaving it to its own devices to find ways of amusing itself like clawing a rug, stealing a ball of wool, chewing an electrical cord, or jumping from one chair to another, it's advisable to buy a rubber mouse or ball with which it can entertain itself.

Kittens that have free access to a terrace or garden will amuse them-selves by running after a butterfly, bug, or leaf. Of course, one could invent a hundred other games with a ball of paper, a cork on a string, or a tassle. Imagination will not be lacking to the patient owner, and the kitten will have peaceful sleep.

The danger is in allowing the kitten to play with something unsafe. It could chew an electrical cord, press its wet nose against an electrical outlet, swallow a pin, eat medicine, get into a drawer and be trapped for hours, or fall from a balcony. A kitten should be looked after and kept far from possible dangers. If it must be left alone, it is best to keep the cat closed in a room free from objects that could harm it.

An adult cat plays less frequently and probably the game changes significantly, manifesting itself more as a reflex or a happy memory. But it's not rare to find older cats happily fighting in playful harmony.

When it's necessary to punish the cat

We've already said that, contrary to the dog, the cat rarely accepts training and education. It is a self-taught cat which behaves according to its own instinct and reflexes. While a dog will not jump on an armchair out of obedience to its owner, the cat will jump up when no one is looking because it wants to do it. Dogs have a need to obey a pack leader, while the relationship between cat and man is a compromise, a taciturn accord valid only for the moment. The cat has no leader.

When it impudently disobeys (and that can be often), *the cat should never be hit* or shown a threatening broom or object even if there is a desire to do so. An exaggerated reprimand with screams and noises could have a traumatic, psychological effect. The cat is incapable of clearly correlating a harsh punishment with the theft of a steak, which it perceives as an ordinary administrative action.

After repeated reprimands from the owner for naughty actions such as a theft in the kitchen, the cat doesn't realize its guilt. If we enter the kitchen in the moment of the misdeed, it will run away to avoid punishment, only to repeat it at the next opportunity.

The owner could make clear to the cat that a certain action is prohibited, but he could never make it perform an act of obedience that would last into the future. It is far from the conditioned reflexes and discipline of the dog. But if a cat had the same temperament as a dog, it wouldn't be a cat.

It may be necessary to discipline a cat. According to the advice of cat-lovers, who perhaps have a bit of time at their disposal, the discipline should be executed in a way that seems to have nothing to do with the owner, almost a diabolical retaliation without identification. Arm yourself with a toy water pistol and squirt the animal in the moment of the misdeed.

But in the same moment in which the cat performs an undesirable action like a theft, an unauthorized possession of a couch, jumping on livingroom tables or into the arms of someone, it's sufficient to yell out, "No." After a long time the cat will decide to behave differently.

Claws are dangerous weapons

It is absolutely necessary to prohibit the cat from pulling out its claws on furniture and upholstery. A scratching post, sold in pet supply shops, should be bought for the house cat. The cat's feet only touch the ground with the flat, cushioned part when walking. Only if the cat lives exclusively in an apartment is it safe to have the nails removed surgically although many animal-lovers consider this inhumane under any circumstances. Declawed cats are banned from all cat shows, and most vets refuse to remove a cat's claws. However, the cat who lives in a house and garden should never have them removed because they permit it to run up a tree or into an open shutter in the face of an aggressive dog or some other danger.

The cat scratches objects that are soft to the touch for two reasons:

The female has less space between the anal opening and the genitals.

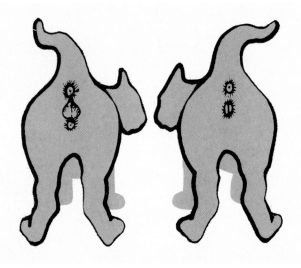

to file its nails and to leave a sign that will be noticed by other cats. It is an indication of propriety and at the same time a kind of public notice that states: "I am here and also disposed to amorous communications."

A house kitten can be taught to smooth its nails on a precise spot, which has already been covered with material: a piece of wood covered with burlap or with an old piece of upholstery. The cat should be placed on the appropriate spot, and it will learn the exercise quickly and with satisfaction and will probably use the pleasant tool even if its life is more often spent outside. Some house cats, however, lose the habit of scratching and the problem solves itself.

Introduction to a new house
We already know that the kitten's separation from its mother and siblings is painless. It was already used to exploring outside of its little dwelling with its restless brothers, imagining that destiny was offering it a new life. And now it becomes the property of a person, very often of a child.

Transport of the kitten to the new house of strange odors should be done in a box punctured for air passage, a proper wicker basket, or a carrier designed for small animals. The box should be sturdy enough to prevent the cat from tearing its way out and escaping. When it is finally free in its new environment, it is wise to immediately offer some nourishment. The first impression is the one that counts. If the kitten seems to be comfortable, it may be invited to play, perhaps with a ball or empty spool.

After it has eaten, played, and received caresses, the memory of its mother will be far away and a little hazy. After a long sleep, it will be taken in by the new things and singular faces that surround it. It will go about the apartment and terrace on uncertain paws and investigate all corners that are still mysterious. But one must slowly organize a schedule for it to eat at the same time as the family, and be able to rest inside a basket with a cushion or cover, a hygienic little home always located in the same secluded spot. Every owner may organize schedules and habits to be impressed upon the cat according to his or her own way.

It is always necessary to be gentle with a cat, but it will probably give its first affections to the person who plays with it and gives it food. It will flee noisy places, things, and people, like loud record players and children.

The kitten doesn't like to be too manipulated or snatched up unexpectedly. The approach should be patient and calm, and since it is sensitive to tones of the voice it should be spoken to sweetly and caressed with prudence. Children like to play with animals, but it should be remembered that cats tire easily and it's not prudent to excite them beyond their limit. When it seeks shelter and its tail is agitated, don't pursue it and leave it to its own business.

If the cat is not well familiarized in its new environment, it may try to run away to its old house, regardless of how far away it is. Use of an identification tag will help a lost or runaway cat to get home. Animal wardens cannot return lost cats or dogs without this.

How to select a cat? Above all, be sure that it is in the best of health.

The importance of the cat bed
It is important that the kitten, as soon as it joins a family, finds its corner already furnished with a basket and cushion. In this way we avoid leaving it to find a bed, armchair, rug, or something comfortable for itself. The owner should do his best to make the new arrival feel right at home. The short period of adjustment, even if comforted by games and good food, is always somewhat traumatic for the cat.

There are some helpful ways to make the kitten feel more secure. If the kitten has been prematurely taken from the mother and it is unsettled and unhappy during its first days in the new habitation, a hot-water bottle (imitating the heat of the mother's body) or a wind-up clock with loud ticks (for the heartbeat of the mother) should be placed in the basket.

There are many choices for setting up a cat bed, from the cat bed sold in specialized shops to the homemade solution of an old wooden box. The size must be in proportion to the size of an average adult cat, realizing that the cat prefers to sleep snuggled up rather than stretched out in a large space. The basket or small drawer should also have sides of about twelve inches so that the kitten feels more secure within the walls and no drafts can be felt. It may also be lined with cloth, straw, or strips of paper, which should be changed periodically to maintain a hygienic place. Cat-owners know well how it loves to hide itself in something that protects it (a cardboard box or drawer or laundry basket) if it doesn't already have its own bed.

On a professional level, breeders keep proper environments furnished with baskets, wire cages, balanced heating, proper hygiene, and peri-

Cats sleep for two-thirds of the day.

odical visits by a vet. But in every part of the world millions of cats exist that don't have any of this, not even food or heat. They're completely poor and live under the stars and clouds, possibly defended by a sloping roof or a damp basement. Sometimes on cold or foggy nights, they creep under the hood of a car and place themselves on top of the motor where a bit of warmth exists.

It is not always true that a cat enjoys a well-prepared basket, which is often stubbornly refused like a spoiled child. The cat may choose to sleep in strange and not very soft places like a wooden chest, among books, on a radiator, or on cool floor tiles on summer days. If we are open-minded and allow the cat to sleep on an armchair, at least cover the object with something that may be washed for hygienic reasons.

The eating place should always be the same, where the animal will not be disturbed by people passing. If there is more than one cat in the house, each should have its own spot to eat separately.

The battle against rats
Cats in ancient Rome found food by catching mice in food warehouses and by successfully battling those more robust and worldly mice that arrived in Italy in the wake of the barbarians. But the large, aggressive rats appeared after the year 1000 A.D., descending from the holds of ships of the Crusaders who were returning from the Orient.

The black rats found their way into homes, and inspired by incredible appetites they entered food depositories, destroying provisions and harvests. From their contact with filth and sewage, the implacable rodents

A kitten taken from its mother will sleep better the first nights with a hot-water bottle, and the ticking of an alarm clock, which will remind it of its mother's heartbeat.

also became carriers of disease. A pair of rats could reproduce fifty to eighty in a year, which in turn quickly begin to procreate at an incredible progression.

It was at this point that merchants decided to import many legions of cats from northern Africa and the Orient. The possession of a cat became a necessity for every civilized family. But its price was very high, because mass reproduction of the cat had still not occurred. In addition, there existed the danger that the useful feline would disappear or be stolen, perhaps for culinary intentions.

The cat was therefore prized in Europe not as a desirable toy, but as the newest and most useful of the domestic animals. We have already spoken of the medieval cruelties. But already in the seventeenth century the French minister Jean Baptiste Colbert actually prescribed that every ship about to depart should have on board at least "two mice-cats."

The legendary hunters
The hunting of a mouse is a profound inclination rooted in the cat. If a cat perceives the closeness of a mouse, it will wait for hours, and after a quiet wavering of its pelvis it will throw itself at the mouse with the swiftness of an arrow.

Even if properly fed, many cats will hunt rodents. It is ready to practice the art of hunting at any hour of the day or night, since it can see at night with very little light. It doesn't pounce on mice out of hunger but rather because of instinct and teaching from the mother cat. A particular cat nicknamed "the great hunter" in the twenty years of its life, is said to have killed more than 22,000 mice. A young and cunning cat in good

The cat will become accustomed to sleeping in its own prepared bed, which should be placed in a quiet spot.

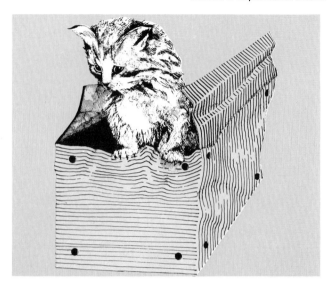

physical and psychological condition could kill at least 1,000 mice in a year. But it should be realized that mice often spontaneously keep away from the houses where cats live.

Robust cats in factories still live with the singular duty of keeping the place free of mice. Especially in warehouses or in food industries, there is the tendency to replace the tested hunter with mousetraps or chemical products. This modern type of extermination is only partially efficient, because mice are very clever animals and they quickly learn to avoid the traps and to recognize the poisoned bait.

Relationships with the dog

The old saying "to fight like cats and dogs" indicates that the two animals are irreconcilable enemies. This expression has lost its veracity.

But dogs and cats, once roaming the countryside without restraints, were the two classic antagonists. Then civilization joined them, and dogs and cats found themselves nose to nose and the dialogue was made possible.

Puppies and kittens began to play together, beginning a peaceful coexistence. If the subjects are still young but already formed, even if the psychology and language of the dog and cat are at opposites, they often find a neutral ground to meet on. They approach each other with caution, and if the disposition of the dog is calm, without unexpected nervous attacks, the cat will slowly accept a friendship.

In order for a good coexistence to occur the character types of both animals play a big part. There are cats and dogs that attack as soon as

Kittens quickly forget their mother and siblings.

they see each other, some ignore each other, some become curious and become friends, and others tolerate each other. The sight of dogs and cats that eat out of the same bowl or sleep in the same bed is rare but not exceptional, even if it is still catalogued among the "curious photos."

The house cat is an untouchable friend for some dogs, but it will protect the cat from intrusions; it can also happen that the cat will defend its dog friend with the same altruism.

The other side of the coin is this: a cat used to living in harmony with a dog places the same complete faith in any other stray dog, ignoring the danger of letting itself get close. Too much confidence is therefore a risk.

There exist dogs that have an atavistic and unstoppable instinct to hunt in their veins, like certain terriers, hounds, and sporting dogs easily excitable in the face of the odor of wild animals. A relationship of co-existence with the cat and these types of dogs will be much more problematic.

Often, however, if dogs concede to a respectful friendship with a house cat, they remain forever enemies with strange cats that happen to venture into their territory.

Very rarely will a cat be the first to instigate an attack on a dog, at least if it's not a question of a female that has just given birth and intends to defend her defenseless offspring.

When it is evident that a dog is getting ready to fight, the cat straightens up, arches itself, and keeps its claws ready. Often, before this

Play behavior is a rehearsal for later adult activities (defense, hunting, sex).

defense reaction is realized, the dog stops itself at some distance and is happy to bark furiously. As soon as possible the cat will make a quick dash in the other direction, finding refuge in places inaccessible to dogs, like the top of a closet, a small window that leads to the garage, the opening to a basement, or the limb of a tree.

The wave of popularity of cats that has covered Europe and America in the last years (it is calculated that in the United States 30 million households have a cat living in them) finds justification in the fact that the feline is a very exalting and seductive animal. It is less bother than a dog, needs less assistance, and can actually take care of itself.

Sexual life
The genitals of the female are in part internal: the uterus, cervix, ovaries and fallopian tubes; and in part external, like the vulva and clitoris. While the uterus of a woman is triangular, that of the feline has a Y-shape, with two long horns and a short, central part. The sexual life of a female cat is controlled either by the ovaries or the brain. The part of the brain is called the hypothalamus and is sensitive to internal and external stimuli, which regulates the cat's temperature, the metabolism of nutrients, sleep, and influences the reproductive processes.

The sexual apparatus of the male is external. The testicles are contained in a sack of skin called the scrotum and become visible when the cat is five weeks old. Those who don't have experience with cats can confuse male with female kittens. Only after two or three months

The kitten is always restless. Its exuberance must be held in check because when playing, some danger, even fatal, may befall it: contact with an electrical wire, remaining imprisoned in a box, swallowing a toxic substance.

do the two testicles begin to take form and appear solid and smooth. The penis of the cat has an intense red color and in erection turns its apex toward the tail. The curved extremity of the penis is covered with imperceptible barbs, which serve to stimulate the female, provoke ovulation, and keep the penis itself in the vagina.

It is not rare that one month after birth there may be a kitten in the litter that has only one testicle, or in some cases a kitten with none. These kittens are often sterile and not accepted in cat shows if both testicles have not dropped. There are, however, categories established at shows with special awards for altered males and spayed females.

Difficult days when in heat

A female cat can whelp three or four times a year if made pregnant. Especially in spring the periods of heat can last from twenty to thirty days, followed by long summer pauses and by a calmer fall resurgence. This uneven distribution of times in heat mainly exists in house cats because of captivity and domestication of the species has altered the rhythm set down by nature.

This period varies from cat to cat and can last from a minimum of three days to a maximum of fifteen. If during the first few days of heat a female cat is impregnated, the period will last only a few days longer.

It is very obvious when a cat is in heat: she becomes more tame and wants to be caressed, rubs her belly on the floor, rolls on the floor with her stomach up, meows with alternate acute yowls, and sometimes seems aggressive. The exterior genitals are swollen, which accompanies a slight loss of good humor.

"Your cat has become thin—beyond being sick, she's in love," wrote the poet Umberto Saba with a light touch.

To avoid pregnancies, especially for cats that live in apartments, it is necessary to keep the female under watch, keeping doors and windows closed especially if they face onto gardens and terraces from which access to roofs is quite easy. As if it were a serenade, some males know how to voice their amorous invitations that the prospective bride accepts with great interest. The female cat should be kept like a prisoner behind kind bars during the brief period of heat in order to avoid the unwanted birth of kittens.

If an owner has a female cat and wants to make her procreate, he can find a proper male either by referring to a breeder who has the same breed, contacting a vet, or advertising in a local paper. It is unadvisable to couple small females with robust males, which could result in difficult pregnancies and births. Do not subject a female to maternity before she reaches one year old.

The drama of sex

In contrast to the female who is very affectionate, the stimulated male is nervous, loses his appetite, flees from caresses, and forgets about the elementary rules of hygiene, which he had always practiced before.

The male becomes excited by the smell of the female, and he follows the trail until he reaches her and then completes the sexual act. Mating between cats can occur up to ten times in one hour and usually up to

The most useful task that a cat fulfills is hunter of mice. Castrated cats do not lose this instinct.

the prostration of the male. But all does not end here because the male can be substituted by another who is waiting. The female will not complain.

Contact of the genitals only lasts ten seconds in the reproductive act. Immediately after the male's ejaculation, the female lets out a sharp yell, followed by a violent separation. This harsh reaction of the female is explained by the fact that the penis has a structure that is capable of causing a painful pull in the vagina.

The males return home after a few days or even weeks when the owners have already given them up for lost. They arrive tired, dirty, hungry, and often wounded by scratches and bites from their rivals or mating partners. Then the deserved period of rest begins.

The sexual development of the female is complete at the age of six to ten months. The male passes the first year in virginity and becomes attracted to females at about one-and-a-half years old.

Cats with short hair have a longer fertile period than those with long hair, lasting until they are ten to eleven years old, but for all cats the period of maximum sexual activity is concentrated between the ages of five to six.

If a cat-owner desires to alter the time when his cats go into heat, for reasons such as having the kittens born in a mild season, he should go to a vet who can inject a hormone that will take care of this. Once the effect of this passes, the cat will return to her normal schedule. This injection cannot be repeated for an unlimited amount of times.

Four cats and two mice in a miniature of Bestiary of Lincoln, *twelfth century.*

cunt. q̄ ex diulis naſcunt. uc mul' ex eq̄ 7 aſi
no. burdo: ex eq̄ ℣ aſina. ſbride ex aſps ℣ poꝛeꝰ.
ꝯ̃riꝰ ex oue ℣ hyrco. oꝰuſino ex capra ℣ arie
te. ſit autem duꝯ gregis.

Freedom—producer of homeless kittens

The courting of the female occurs with the musical—but not always pleasant—cries of the male. There is usually more than one male, however, and after some fighting, the female chooses the strongest, most pleasing, and most enterprising of her suitors.

In the moment of possession, the male squeezes the female with his claws and bites her nape. If the female then mates with other males, a litter of kittens will be born whose coloring will resemble the palate of a painting after two months, but it may also happen that the kittens are born with only one color.

A purebred female, if mated with a mixed-breed male, will give birth to mixed-breed kittens like the father. But the female who returns home and is later mated with a male of her breed will give birth to purebred kittens.

The female is fertile from the third day of heat. At any time after the third day she could become pregnant. If the mating is done at home or arranged by a professional breeder, the male usually stays with the female for one day and one night. If the male and female come from the same breed but from different owners, an agreement can be reached either by a sum of money or by dividing the litter up. The price should be fixed and a contract signed before the mating takes place.

Norms for those who want to breed

In the last decades, the breeding of purebred cats was organized on a commercial scale that was previously known only in the dog world. In

The old saying "fight like cats and dogs" is losing its veracity: many cases exist where cats and dogs live happily together in the same house or yard.

Usually the most active mating period is in the spring, which lessens in the summer, and starts up again with moderate intensity in the autumn and winter.

A Siamese cat in heat welcomes the attention of a male of the same breed.

the past, breeding cats was considered an unprofitable business because of the great expense involved in arranging matings plus the high cost of space, equipment, medical attention, food, pharmaceuticals and, in some instances, skilled personnel.

The popularity of the domestic cat has grown to gigantic proportions throughout the world, but especially in the United States. The interest in exotic breeds has risen significantly and captured the attention of commercial and nonprofit breeders as well as retailers of livestock. It is now possible to produce any imaginable breed of cat and expect to find prospective customers.

But do not be deceived. Mating cats for a fee and selling kittens is not a profitable business for the average cat-owner. It is not as simple as getting a male and female cat together. Skill, knowledge, and long-term dedication are required to produce genetically sound, breed-stabilized cats. Breeders must develop a reputation for competency and reliability, as they are liable for the quality of kittens they produce and sell. Dedicated breeders/exhibitors are fortunate if they recover their many costs when they balance their ledgers at the end of the year.

The price of kittens varies from breed to breed. Producing an uncommon breed of cat will fetch more money but will also cost more to produce. Stud fees are higher for rare breeds, and in many cases a general knowledge of genetics is required as well as the genetics for that breed. In some breeds it is impossible to mate a male and female specimen and produce kittens that are true in color and type without introducing another breed in the line. This is called *outcrossing*. It is especially true of such breeds as the tailless Manx.

The price of kittens is also influenced by the quality of its pedigree. Obviously, kittens descended from cats with champion and grand champion titles are more valuable than cats with no such distinctions. Being in distinguished show cats is not only prestigious but also indicates the probability of producing distinguished kittens. It should be clear that the business of selling or mating cats is complex and not very profitable for the inexperienced amateur.

Many years of experience are needed to breed cats. The six principal rules for a sure beginning are the following:

1. The male and female must come from the same breed and should be pedigreed.

2. They must be in perfect health and have the proper vaccinations prescribed by vets.

3. They must be of full sexual maturity: one-and-a-half years for females, two years for males. (See individual breeds.)

4. Females of a small size shouldn't be coupled with large males.

5. Never mate an inexperienced male with an inexperienced female.

6. Mate a female with a male only if she has already been in heat three times and both are in perfect physical health.

For purebred cats registered with a cat association, a declaration of the match with names and dates should be sent to the proper organization accompanied with the pertinent registration information regarding both cats and the ensuing kittens.

And after sixty days...

After two cats are mated, three weeks must pass before it is certain that the female is pregnant. The vet can confirm it by the palpation of the womb. It is important to palpate the womb of the mother professionally, otherwise the fetus could be damaged and also cause an abortion.

Meanwhile, the female's teats become pink and the fuzz that surrounds them slightly diminishes. The change will be more evident in a first pregnancy; the teats ordinarily are very white and unpronounced.

If the date of the mating is unknown, it is very difficult to predict with any certainty the approximate date of the birth. If it is not really necessary, do not subject the pregnant cat to X-rays.

To be certain that the pregnancy is well under way, at about the fifth week the cat should be brought to the vet where, in addition to the palpating of the womb, he will prescribe proper care, either with medicine or food, to assure that the litter is born healthy and properly nourished with full maternal efficiency.

The pregnancy has an average duration of sixty-three to sixty-six days (about nine weeks), taking into consideration variations of the breed, as in the case of Siamese cats that prolong the term as much as ten weeks, or the climate, the size of the cat, the body's system, or the type of nourishment. If there are many fetuses, the term may be shorter.

If, however, the normal sixty-three to sixty-six days pass without symptoms of an imminent birth, a vet should be called. A Caesarean section is necessary for some cats, an operation no longer dangerous provided that a hasty decision is not taken.

A spontaneous abortion is very rare in the cat. A typical sign is hem-

The male and female protect the litter from danger.

Gestation period is usually eight to nine weeks. Cats have litters of three to five kittens, with a maximum of six.

orrhaging. In this case the cat should be placed in a warm and quiet place, consoled with caresses and a vet called immediately.

It is dangerous to submit the pregnant cat to medicines and vaccinations. One example: the antibiotic used against ringworm may cause deformities in kittens. Never give any medicine to a pregnant cat without the instructions of a vet.

During the pregnancy, a cat in good health should be happy, hungry, affectionate, without pain, and practice normal hygienic functions. She should spend calm days in a clean environment. Let the cat move around and play because a pregnant cat is not sick.

She shouldn't get fat so her food should be of substance, but not in excess. A slim cat in good form should not have difficulty in giving birth. The diet should be altered to a daily allowance of five to six ounces of meat, but the quantity of starches should be diminished. Milk and cheese—foods rich in calcium—can contribute to the skeletal formation and supply lost vitamins and minerals to the pregnant cat. Also, a spoonful or two of boiled vegetables will help the intestines to function.

Preparing for the birth
While waiting for the birth, long-haired cats must be brushed more than usual to prevent the cat from swallowing hairs when cleaning herself, which could create hairballs and obstruct the intestinal functions during this delicate period.

If the cat should suffer from constipation, a spoonful of prescribed oil

Birth in a drawer: not a very appropriate place for the happy event.

or a light laxative should be administered every five to six days in doses recommended by a veterinarian. Anything stronger could cause worse damage and in some cases be the cause of a miscarriage.

A few days before the happy event, the teats should be lubricated with some vaseline to make them smoother for when the hungry kittens arrive.

The cat may show some difficulty in cleaning her anal region because of her enlarged stomach. In this case, it is necessary to gently wash the cat's intimate parts with warm water.

Some days before the birth select a resting place with a special bed consisting of a box about two feet square and two feet high with a window cut into the side twelve inches from the bottom, so that after two weeks the kittens cannot easily climb out. At the bottom of the box, place a blanket and soft cushion made of a towel that can be changed daily.

This box (or basket) should then be placed in a quiet corner of the house, where the light coming from a window or overhead lamp will regularly enter for warmth. The cat, in the meantime, will get accustomed to the new bed, so that at the moment of birth, when she's a bit frightened by the events, she will not hastily choose an armchair, sofa, or a closet full of clothes. Place a litter pan near the nest a week or two before the birth.

Don't allow the cat to give birth in the garage, cellar, or even the backyard. Deter her from going out of the house to prevent her from giving birth in an inappropriately cold place. Cats, as a species, have a

A Devon Rex feeding her kittens.

strong potential for survival, but don't forget that in the first days of life a different mortality rate is registered.

The birth of the kittens
The cat understands when the moment of giving birth is near. She begins to appear agitated and meows in a strange way, sweet and musical, a kind of request for help and response to what is approaching. She anxiously seeks a quiet corner but seems dissatisfied. The owner should place her near the prepared box and begin to caress her with a light touch on her head and womb, helping her to remain calm with affectionate words. For centuries cats have given birth without the help of anyone and instinctively know what to do. They handle it very well, but they'll appreciate the close presence of a friendly voice.

To be sure if the moment of birth is about to take place, the cat's anal temperature should be taken every day after the sixtieth day of pregnancy. The normal temperature is between 101° to 102.5° (38° to 39°C). If it is a little lower, the happy event will soon take place. Another significant indication is found when the teats begin to produce milk.

The abdominal muscles will contract, the skin of the sides will be taut, the external genitals will swell, and the rate of respiration will increase. The cat will either assume a stretched-out position or squatted one as if to defecate. Within fifteen minutes the first kitten will appear in the placental sac. It is about two to three inches long and looks like a little fat mouse. Between one expulsion and another a few minutes or an

Sometimes the newborn cannot breathe because of mucus that is obstructing the respiratory passages. The kitten should be held with its head face down for a few minutes to facilitate the expulsion of the mucus.

hour may pass, so that even a prolonged interval should not be cause for concern.

A cat gives birth to an average of four to five kittens but sometimes only one. Cases of a six- to seven-kitten litter are rare. A litter of twelve kittens was once recorded. Being rather prolific animals, a female may give birth to about fifteen kittens a year. If allowed to reproduce freely, the geometric progression indicates that mountains of felines could be created. We shall speak later of the advantages of neutering.

If the birth occurs a week or two prematurely, be prepared to lose all or part of the litter since premature kittens have a low survival rate.

It is important that the room where the cat will give birth is warm. A cold and humid environment may cause hypothermia in newborn kittens that are not yet capable of regulating their body temperature, so the cold may kill them.

If the cat is giving birth for the first time, frightened by the pain, she might not manage to bite off the umbilical cord. It is necessary to intervene in such a case. Tie the cord with clean thread or dental floss a half-inch to an inch from the body and with sterilized scissors cut the cord gently above the thread.

The kittens come out with the placenta (a mass rich in blood that forms in the uterus and serves to give nourishment to the fetus) trailing behind them. The kitten is in an amniotic sac with the umbilical cord attached to the other end of the placenta. The mother will immediately

The female cat is a devoted and courageous mother.

free each one from the sac, lick it, clean it, and gently dry it. The continuous licking stimulates the respiration of the kitten, which will begin to get restless and cry for the first time in a world that it still doesn't see.

The mother cat swallows the placentae, the umbilical cords, and also the first excrements of her young. The hygiene now is fully demonstrated, so that the towel in the box remains stained only by some spots of blood, the only residue of the birth. The act of consuming the placentae and the other waste probably derives from the primitive instinct of removing odors and traces of a bloody nature to avoid the arrival of potential predators.

After all of the kittens have been born, the mother will need to rest. She should be left in semi-darkness together with her small tribe. Remember to put a little light food next to her, a cup of water, and her clean litter pan. In this way, at the first necessity, she won't have to go far away and abandon the young, which will soon be asking for their first meal.

A cat can comfortably nurse five kittens if she has had good nourishment during the pregnancy. But if the babies are numerous, it may be necessary to help the mother with specially designed bottles and commercially prepared milk substitutes. Do not feed newborns with cows' milk. If the milk amount is weak, the veterinarian may intervene with a product that aids secretion so that there will be milk for everyone.

The mother cat may have a light red discharge after giving birth. This may last about one week. A bright red or greenish discharge in large

Self-grooming is a kitten's birthright.

amounts requires professional attention. It could indicate internal bleeding or infection caused by a retained placenta.

The newborn kitten

Like most mammals, kittens at birth are blind, deaf, and without teeth. It is normal for their eyes to remain closed for eight to ten days. If at the moment of birth the eyes are open, some malformations to the ocular globe may occur with serious consequences. Healthy eyes begin to see well when the kitten is about one month old.

As soon as they're born, kittens shouldn't be touched by strange hands. Certain mothers may be disturbed by the different odor, and she may not recognize the kitten as her own and refuse to feed it.

The first milk that the mother offers her young is called *colostrum* and is made of fats, casein, lactose, and various nutrients. It is high in antibodies. The milk, in addition to providing light nutritional needs, cleans the digestive channel of the newborn and initiates the future intestinal activity.

After being carried around for two weeks, the kitten will begin to walk and coordinate its movements. On the twentieth day it will sit down, at twenty-five days it will touch objects with its paws, and at one month it will attempt to clean itself.

The amount of love that a mother provides her young varies in the animal kingdom, but that of the feline is exceptional. Not even the detractors can deny that the cat is a devoted and courageous mother.

Even though it is an extremely rare event, it can happen that a mother demonstrates a tendency to devour her offspring. In this unnatural act the mother sees the kittens as prey or is redirecting aggression. If it is possible to rescue the kittens, dry them with a warm cloth and draw them near to the teats again only at the moment of feeding, remaining to watch them. The contact of the young with the teats will give pleasure to the mother, so that she'll be able to accept the whole litter and begin to care for and love them.

The bold mothers

The stray cat is an excellent mother. She will try to give birth in a corner where she can eventually defend herself from the curiosity of dogs and children. If at night or during the day she must avoid some danger, she will transfer her litter from one hiding place to another, grasping the young one by one at the neck, cleaning them, feeding them, but never abandoning them. Every need of the kitten is satisfied. When the first teeth come out, the mother will teach her kitten to hunt little animals, to play, and to feed itself. She is the nourisher and master of life.

Mixed-breed kittens can be miniatures of the mother or father, or a mixture of both. If they look like only one parent, they have the so-called unilateral heredity. If they resemble both, they have a bilateral heredity. But genetics are rich in fantasy. The young can clearly resemble their grandparents and great grandparents. From a white female and gray male can be born a red offspring. This is a matter of genetics. Kittens from the same litter can also come out differently—a sign that the mother mated with more than one male.

Usually a house cat, purebred or mixed breed, undergoes an attentive control by her owners when she is in heat. Except when she disappears from sight, the owner almost always manages to prevent the female from meeting with a male that is waiting behind the door.

If, however, the cat enjoys her liberty and always returns to the family with new and undesirable litters, it is advisable to consider surgical sterilization. This will avoid the preoccupation of having the kittens end up in uncertain hands; or put down.

Forty to sixty days of nursing

According to the plan of mother nature, the nursing of the little ones will last for an average of forty to sixty days. The mother cat's milk is very rich in protein, fat, vitamins, and minerals, and the kitten will double its birth weight in eight days. Only the rabbit grows more quickly than the cat.

To survive, the kittens must take their first milk as soon as possible. The mother will encourage them to nourish themselves a few minutes after the birth, lying on her side, pointing and guiding their mouths delicately toward the teats. But as all mammals, kittens also are piloted by an innate instinct that steers them toward finding food immediately from the correct fountain.

After every nursing, the kittens will fall asleep and the mother will take advantage of the time to feed herself, take a walk, or clean herself. But she always remains attentive to the meowing of her offspring and is

A litter of white kittens asking for affection.

punctual in returning to the familial box when it is time for the next feeding.

During the two months of nursing, the mother cat needs a rather substantial diet. It should be remembered that liquid nourishment like broth, milk, and soup will help the milk flow. But along with the liquids, the mother should also be obtaining calcium, phosphorous, protein, vitamins A and D derived from meat (cut up), fish, cheese, and egg yolk. A variety of dishes should be offered during the course of a week, dividing them into three meals a day. Fattening foods and leftovers from the table with bones should be avoided.

Artificial nursing
Although it happens rarely, a cat may suffer complications at birth or some other difficulty. She may remain without milk or refuse to nurse her young.

In all of these cases, artificial nursing should be administered. If the mother hasn't lost all of her milk, mixed nursing, that is, some from the mother and some artificial, would be the best for the survival of the kittens. But often completely artificial nursing is necessary.

Since cow's milk is unadaptable for kittens in the first weeks, they should be fed with particular, artificial milk for small animals or with a product recommended by a veterinarian. The dosage will be determined by a vet, who will also prescribe a prepared antibiotic substitute of immunized antibodies against feline illnesses which are contained in the cat's milk.

A good nourishment for kittens may also be prepared with a pint of *(opposite) Meals should become increasingly enriched: milk, then milk with egg yolk, then several tablespoons of minced chicken or homogenized veal.*

(below) Administering artificial milk may be accomplished by the use of a plastic dropper or by a special bottle for cats.

condensed milk, an egg yolk, and 4 tsp. of sugar. A teaspoonful should be given to every kitten seven to eight times a day for the first three weeks.

When feeding a kitten with a commercial formula, the person performing the task must be very patient and constant. The hoped-for results are not always obtained. It should be administered with a plastic eyedropper or with a syringe (without the needle) or with a small feeder for cats, which is sold in specialty shops on which the proper dosage for each feeding is written.

The formula should be warm at 100°F (38°C) and always allow the kitten to suck on its own, without solicitation, which could result in suffocation. When it falls asleep or when it emits bubbles of milk from its mouth, which indicates that it is not sucking anymore, it has had its fill.

The seven to eight feedings in the twenty-four-hour period will have the longest interval during the night (five to six hours). During the course of the weeks of feeding, the number of nursings will be reduced and the quantity will increase, until weaning time.

Becoming carnivorous

Weaning is the passing from an exclusively milk diet to a mixed one. It is initiated at about the third or fourth week, separating the kittens from the teats for the time necessary to put the new food on a plate.

If the kittens remain too long with the mother, they become retarded in their growth, attempting to suck even when the mother no longer has

any milk. It is not rare that a one- or two-year-old cat, when held in a person's arms, will start to claw at the edge of its owner's clothing, looking for its mother's teat.

Very often a newborn kitten will be lost before a plate full of milk. What is this new thing? In this case, it is necessary to bring the kitten close to the plate, delicately placing its nose near and putting a drop of milk on its lips. It will immediately be attracted to it and lick the milk. Its hunger will teach it the lesson, and it will soon begin to lick the plate on its own.

Meals should then become more substantial: from the first milk, then milk with an egg yolk, to a few spoonfuls of chicken and veal, to some chopped liver, to broth with meat finely cut, and then to real meat (chicken, fish, or giblets, cut up into small pieces).

It may happen that during the weaning some kittens may develop intestinal problems. Milk with a few spoonfuls of warm camomile tea should be substituted immediately. The kitten will surely not like it, so it should be given in drops from the side of its mouth as if it were medicine. If diarrhea should persist, a veterinarian should be consulted, particularly if a bad odor is present.

Sometimes a wet nurse is needed

If the mother dies or for some reason disappears, in addition to milk the kitten often lacks protection and warmth. In this sad situation, it is advisable to maintain the orphaned kitten in an environment of 85° to 90°F

Part of the kitten's early behavior is play and mutual grooming.

(32°C) for the first week; in the following two weeks, the temperature may go down to 80°F (26°C); at about the fourth week reduce the temperature to 70°F (22°C).

The problem may be solved with an electric incubator or the use of a heating pad regulated by a thermometer placed inside the box where the newborns live. Drafts may be fatal to the kittens and may easily cause pneumonia.

Kittens without a mother, fed and kept warm by artificial means, may be retarded in their growth. Also in this case the veterinarian can prescribe the necessary cures.

It is useful for the psychological development of kittens to have contact with other adult felines. If there is another cat in the house that has just given birth, the orphans could be joined with the other litter. Cats don't know how to count, but the addition of new kittens should take place when the adoptive mother is absent. The orphaned kittens, in contact with the others, will assume the odor of them, so that when the mother returns to her fold, she won't notice any difference and will treat the adopted ones as if they were her own.

If there is no other cat in the house that has just given birth, the best advice is to ask a veterinarian. He is in contact with many people who are trying to get rid of newborns, and he may know of a cat that has just given birth and still has milk to give. Once weaned, the kittens may return home.

The kitten begins to feed itself.

Kittens fed only by humans can have difficulty in their bodily functions because the mother licks them to stimulate these functions. If this problem persists for three to four days, it is best to consult a veterinarian.

Good-bye to the mother without tears
At about forty to fifty days old, the kitten begins to feed itself, tastes new things, is curious about everything that moves, plays, and confronts life independently. The mother has finished her work of teaching her young. Now she is tired of having these children, which still bite at her teats for milk at intervals, even though they are fat, round, and roaming about.

There will not be tormenting good-byes. It is best to make the separation when the mother is outside or eating. But even if after eleven or twelve weeks it happens in her presence, she won't display any possessive reaction. Take one kitten away at a time on different days, so as to slowly habituate the mother's return to her normal life without the worry of the reckless little ones.

If after some months she meets her young, the mother won't recognize them; once grown up, the kittens will consider their mother a nice cat, but a stranger.

In the meantime, the developed kitten has become a hearty eater. Try to vary its diet quite often, but pay attention to the schedule. After weaning, there should be four meals given at 8:00 A.M., noon, 5:00 P.M., and 9:00 P.M. At five months old, give one meal at 8:00 A.M., 1:00 P.M., and 7:00 P.M. From eight months to a year there should be meals at 8:00 A.M. and 5:00 P.M. (or when the family eats dinner). An adult cat needs to be fed two meals a day or one abundant meal a day, best given in the late afternoon.

A young cat between five and seven months old will need 2 to 3 oz. (56 to 84g) of meat per day, also some rice, milk, corn flakes and cooked pieces of vegetables. Cooked fish is a well-known delicacy for the cat, which would do anything to have it. Attracted by its odor, it is capable of snatching it off a table. But during its earlier years, it is enough to serve it once a week, always without bones. The growth of the kitten will be enhanced by a quality vitamin supplement prescribed by a veterinarian.

A purebred cat is usually fortunate enough to live in a comfortable house and be taken care of by considerate owners. And as with all things that are expensive, the cat will be treated well: regular meals, a basket for sleeping, combings, and even a collar. And, of course, it will receive a lot of affection.

But mixed breed cats are mostly lucky and meet up with owners that love and care for them independently from their slight nobility. When giving away kittens born of a house cat, try to be somewhat sure that they'll be appreciated and well-treated.

A cat is a wonderful companion, a personage to admire, enjoyable at every hour of the day, but he who buys or receives it from someone must realize that its presence in the house requires responsibility and sacrifice. It should not be taken on with easy enthusiasm or with the idea of having it play with children. Parents may sometimes buy pets for their children that are soon neglected once the initial delight has passed.

Too many cats? Neutering

The first birth of kittens at home usually occurs with satisfaction, anxiety, curiosity, even doubts. Finding new homes for the newborn kittens can be difficult enough to accomplish. But at the second birth, neither friends, relatives, nor shopkeepers will be disposed to accepting another cat.

The indirect ways of preventing a pregnancy, among them deodorants, do not yield effective results on cats because sexual attraction is based more on behavior and meowing and less on odorous signals, which is the case with dogs. To avoid having many litters born in a year, surgical sterilization should be considered, that is, spaying (the removal of the ovaries in a female) and castration (the removal of the testicles in the male). The removal of the ovaries eliminates the period of heat and fecundity. Tying of the tubes is not usually done because even though if renders the cat sterile, it doesn't eliminate its ability to go into heat.

Some people consider sterilization an act against nature, and propose as an alternative the segregation of the female during the period of heat. But a cat normally left to freely go about the house, terrace, and garden will not usually accept two weeks of prison without scratching and calling out day and night. Other serenades will be going on in the street. And at the first open door, the cat will run out in search of a mate.

Others allow the cat to be left free and then eliminate the kittens after birth. But this form of euthanasia is quite dramatic and cruel, especially

if the kittens become conscious. In addition, the mother will suffer from the accumulation of unused milk without her young.

According to the experience of experts, spaying of the female is a better option. The decision should be made as soon as possible when the cat is still young, between six and seven months, before the first heat or after the first pregnancy. It is an operation without dangers that is given under total anesthesia and is part of the normal surgical routine of all veterinarians specializing in small animals.

The female should not be operated on when in heat because her reproductive organs are then larger and more active and could thus cause complications. After a few days, the stitches are removed and the animal returns to its normal condition. Castration of the male is a less complicated procedure and requires less time with the veterinarian.

The operation gives tranquility to both the owner and his cat. After the sterilization the cat will maintain affections for the house and family, and will even become more serene.

Of course, breeders and those who desire to produce offspring from their purebred cat to sell the kittens or have them participate in shows should avoid spaying.

If an increase in weight is noticed in sterilized cats, male or female, reduction of their daily food intake by 30 percent is advisable.

The castrated male cat is less troublesome, stays more at home, lives longer, and its urine loses its characteristic bad odor. The instinct to hunt mice remains in the castrated cat, but it will be more serene and affectionate. It usually won't gain weight and become lazy.

A male cat should be castrated when his testicles are visible. If it is

A cat should receive a varied and balanced diet.

done too soon, the operation may stunt his growth, alter his voice, or cause a small head and weak claws. The castration is done under total anesthesia, is less complicated than the neutering of a female, and does not present the danger of hemorrhaging or infections. Obviously, this intervention should be reserved for males that are not intended to be reproducers.

Let us remember: a male that runs out of the house irresponsibly contributes to the increase of kittens. Owners of female cats run the risk of finding themselves periodically with a litter in the house.

Feeding: a difficult client
The cat is born a carnivorous animal and has fundamentally remained this way. For centuries, it fed itself on mice, birds, snakes, frogs, lizards, grasshoppers, crickets, and squirrels. Today, any kind of meat has remained its favorite food.

In its wild state, the cat fed on living prey, which was consumed whole, furnishing it with a complete plate of nutrition. The cat not only ate the muscular part of the killed animal but also the bones, entrails, and the digestive tubes. So sometimes it's necessary to reinvigorate its past as hunter by providing it with a meal of entire pieces of chicken or veal.

The main thing to remember in regard to a cat's nutrition is that it has nothing in common with the dog. The dog, like man, is omnivorous, that is, it eats meat, vegetables, fruit, breads, and processed foods. The cat is a lion in miniature, with a mouth, jaws, and teeth adapted for devouring whole animals.

The cat remains fundamentally carnivorous.

Cats need a diet of twice as much protein when compared with dogs. Only meat, fish, eggs, milk, and all byproducts of animal organs can satisfy these ancestral needs. More fats are also required by cats and are important to their diet. Besides providing vitamins A, D, and E, these products supply the cat with the correct quantity of calcium and phosphorous.

Milk, although a good source of calcium, is not usually tolerated by some adult cats, which cannot digest the sugars in the milk and may cause diarrhea.

The easiest and most secure system of feeding a cat is with special canned, soft-moist, or dry cat food, which contains protein, fat, carbohydrates, vitamins, and minerals. These foods should be labeled "complete" or "balanced" on the can or box.

The domestic cat, however, having lived near human food has slowly adjusted to try a bit of everything. Through the centuries, it has become necessary for the cat to modify its eating habits to be able to eat human food, which is more varied and less concentrated than pure meat. Its intestines have gradually lengthened to seven feet or more as compared with the wild cat, whose intestine is five feet.

Keeping the cat at the right weight
Regardless of the cat's breed, they all fall within the same range of size and weight. Their way of life is basically the same so that a general diet may be applied to all cats.

The list of foods

The following is a quick examination of the principal foods for the feeding of cats.

Meat: The cat likes any kind of meat. 3 oz. (84g) of beef with a moderate portion of fat provides 330 calories. The cat loves fat. Meat may be given raw but is safer if slightly cooked and cut into little pieces.

Fish: The cat can smell cooked fish from far away. It is nutritious, digestible, and rich in phosphorous. Three ounces of fish corresponds to 140 calories. Bones should always be removed.

Chicken: 2 to 8 oz. (56 to 224g) of boned chicken breast provides 160 calories. It is an appetizing meat of medium caloric value, easily digested. Since owner's often have it at their own table, cats eat it frequently. Bones again should be meticulously removed.

Organs: Internal organs of animals are enjoyed by cats. But one must exercise caution. Liver, for example, rich in vitamins and protein, may produce the effect of a laxative. 3 oz. (84g) of liver provides 195 calories. Lungs are low in calories, so they may be given when the cat needs to lose weight. Tripe, cut up into small pieces, could be given weekly as a variant to the normal meals.

Cheese: 1 oz. (28g) of processed American cheese provides 105 calories and is an excellent food. But it is very fattening. Therefore, only small amounts should be given along with another light food. Fermented cheeses, such as feta and bleu, should be avoided.

Milk: This is rich in calcium and should be occasionally given only to cats that like it and can easily digest it. If it causes diarrhea, it should be avoided.

Vegetables: These should be mixed with meat, cooked, and cut up in small quantities. They aid digestion and provide fiber. Some cats especially like asparagus. Do not give them potatoes.

Soup: Broth with meat and vegetables, pasta, and rice mixed with pieces of meat or cheese is very good.

Canned food: This can be given without hesitation. There is a wide range of choices offered. Alternating canned food with kibble is wise.

Cereals: Rice, pasta, and wheats are important suppliers of energy to be given in very limited quantities mixed with meat, but don't give it to cats that are already overweight.

A typical outdoor cattery.

A neutered male house cat should consume 7.5 oz. (210g) of solid food a day. Of this, about 2 oz. (56g) should be of meat while the remainder may be of fat or oil, broth, greens, cheese, or carbohydrates. Larger (or unaltered) cats with a more active daily life should take in more food, up to 8.5 oz. (238g) per day.

The cat knows how to regulate its own hunger and doesn't devour food like a dog. If it doesn't feel like eating or its stomach is bloated it will leave a half-full plate and walk away. If, on the other hand, it is still hungry it will ask for more with an insistent meow.

If the owner's leftovers are used to feed it, all small bones, spices, and sauces must be removed. The food must be given warm or at room temperature, not hot from the pan or cold from the refrigerator. It is best to feed the cat at the same times every day. In this way, it isn't necessary to call the cat to eat because it will know automatically.

Even though the cat can chew well, its food should be cut up into pieces or into strips in a way that it may exercise its teeth and strengthen its jaws. For an older cat, however, very small pieces of meat or soft cheese should be given. The jaws of a feline cannot move laterally but only move up and down. While observing the cat as it eats, note how it moves its head in jerky movements to avoid having the food drop out of its mouth.

The quantity of food it needs depends on its age, weight, individual exercise, and appetite. But the owner should try to keep his cat at a normal weight, especially pampered house cats. It is difficult to recognize the proper weight: one practical suggestion is to touch its ribs—if they cannot be felt, it is a definite sign of obesity.

If the cat is constipated or because it just had a snack, it often will not eat its regular, prepared meal. The food should be left out for about an hour and then put away for use the next day. Water should always be left out in a bowl and changed a few times a day.

The cat is equipped with the ability to understand the purpose of a series of small objects. It can learn the differences between a plate for meat-fish-cheese, a bowl of milk and soup, and another bowl for water. A cat drinks only a little, but it is necessary always to have some water out for it, otherwise it will quench its thirst from a flower vase, sink, fish tank, etc.

The contortionist of hygiene
The cat loves to maintain a very clean body. It practices the teaching of its mother who always lovingly licked it. Its coat is shiny and without odors. Some cat-lovers even say that they themselves are covered with a very nice "perfume of cat."

But this constant hygienic activity, especially of long-haired cats, can be dangerous to the digestive tract. Wetting its body with saliva for hours during the day, the cat swallows a large quantity of hair, so much so that its stomach can have balls of fur form, causing painful obstructions, an arrest of appetite, and consequently a loss of weight. Sometimes these accumulated hairballs can be the cause of a cat's death. When these disturbances to digestion are suspected, it is indispensable to administer a spoonful or two of petroleum jelly for a few days, observing the effects on the feces. But there are also commercial products available

Cats spend a great deal of time cleaning themselves, licking every part of their bodies for which their tongues are so adept.

that, given regularly, relieve the cat from this bothersome inconvenience.

It would be advantageous to grow some grass that the cat could spontaneously eat to induce the passage of these small, disturbing masses. When constipation due to the clogging of hair is evident, a veterinarian should be consulted immediately. But with the foresight of daily brushing, many complications can be avoided. A modest amount of hair intake is not harmful. The regular cleanings assume an important role for the cat, because it is a mirror of its tranquility. A restless or sick cat refuses to clean itself.

The work of combing and brushing
The cat must become used to the owner's hand, which should brush it from the time it is a kitten. Its hair should be brushed and combed periodically and more frequently at the change of seasons. The cat is more receptive to a brushing if it is done during a nap.

In addition to hindering possible intestinal problems, a brushing will avoid having thousands of cat hairs throughout the house and on clothing. Combs with small, close teeth should be used for short hair and those with large teeth for long hair. Hard and soft brushes may be found. Natural bristles are better because synthetic ones like nylon may form electricity and cause the hairs to break. With knotted coats it is necessary to untangle with lotion and fingers. Comb and then brush delicately.

Pay close attention to the skin of the cat, making sure that it looks healthy and not invaded by fleas and ticks. The inspection is very important, especially if the cat has been off wandering and in contact with stray cats.

When licking its coat, the cat may swallow large hairballs. To avoid intestinal occlusions, regularly brush the coat well.

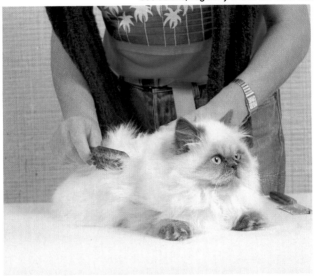

Cat fleas are different from dog fleas. Fleas derive nourishment from blood meals obtained from the host animal. Sometimes their bites cause infections and, if there are many of them, the cat may suffer from anemia. Fleas can live for more than one year in the coat of an animal. Powders and sprays recommended by a veterinarian will be very useful to shorten that all too comfortable and long life of the flea.

Giving a bath
The cat is a clean animal, but in certain cases it needs the help of its owner. If they roam about roofs and gardens, they often enter the house with a dirty coat. Some cats often sleep under cars and get spots of motor oil on their coats. It is not exactly true that cats should never be washed. The cat which has never been bathed has a great mistrust of water. So it should be habituated to washings from a young age; after the second or third time it will be accustomed to contact with water and soap and will accept the inevitable.

It is advisable to bathe the cat in a basin because the size of a large tub could frighten the cat and induce it to pull out its nails to run away out of fear of slipping. Place a rubber mat or towel on the bottom of the basin. It should be half full of warm water with a small quantity of baby shampoo or a commercial shampoo for cats. A "tearless" cat shampoo is recommended.

The cat should then be dried thoroughly, rubbing the towel against its skin. Eventually, a regular hair dryer can be used as long as the cat doesn't get frightened of it and run away.

A careful cleaning of the coat is fundamental not only for the cat's beauty but also for its health.

It is the rare cat that enjoys being washed and immersed in water. But since it is sometimes necessary to subject the cat to a complete bathing, it is best to accustom the cat to this bath at the earliest age possible.

In case the cat has a chronic aversion to a bath, a dry-cleaning may be substituted by sprinkling the coat with baby talcum powder, which absorbs impurities, then brushing well. A commercial "dry shampoo" may also be used.

If the coat is dirtied by tar, grease, car oil, or other substances difficult to remove, drench the spot in mineral oil for twenty-four hours, then wash with soap and water. But when removal of greasy dirt is impossible, it may be necessary to cut some of the hair.

Cleaning the ears and eyes

During a brushing or bath, take the opportunity to examine the cat well and provide a more detailed hygiene. Take advantage of the occasion to clean the inside of the ears with a Q-tip lightly moistened with rubbing alcohol. The alcohol cleanses and then immediately evaporates without leaving a trace of dampness.

The eyes, when irritated by dust or mucous, should be cleansed with a cotton ball moistened with water, lightly passing it over from the inner side to the outside of the face.

Whenever bodily irritants are noted, either of the eye, the ear, scabs on the head, parasites, etc., it's best to bring the cat to a veterinarian. At the veterinarian's also its teeth and gums will be checked and a full exam may be provided. The ear canal contains some wax the color of honey, without odor; if however a bad odor is detected, it could be an indication of an infection or ear mites.

The litter box

The cat is an animal that covers up its excrement, which is an atavistic habit of felines to cover their tracks and odors in order to impede any aggressive act on the part of its enemies. Therefore, the house cat needs its personal "bathroom," that is, a rectangular box of a size that will hold the cat and allow it to cover its feces. It is referred to as a litter box. Place the box in a remote spot such as the bathroom or basement.

Pet supply shops sell plastic boxes for this purpose. Try to avoid using wooden boxes that absorb and hold bad odors. Sand, saw dust, strips of paper, peat, or cat litter, which may be bought at stores in large bags, should be placed at the bottom.

Although it happens rarely, the cat may relieve itself in some prohibited corner of the house. In this case, the spot should be cleaned with ammonia and an odor neutralizer so that the discourtesy is not repeated. To hit a cat is a completely useless punishment that will in no way correct its misbehavior.

On a leash like a dog

Light collars, perhaps with a small bell, may be attached to house cats. The collar shouldn't be rigid like those for dogs, but soft, elastic, and not too loose around the neck to avoid getting caught in some protruding object. A tag with the owner's address may be attached to the collar.

Some types of cats, like the Siamese and Abyssinian, will tolerate being taken out on a leash if they've been accustomed to it from the time they were young. In such cases, it is best to buy a cat harness, which is wrapped around the chest rather than attached to the neck, because if the cat is frightened by something it may be able to slip out of the collar.

Signs when a cat is sick

Naturally, even a house cat can get sick. Viruses and bacteria get into the house in a hundred ways, primarily on the soles of shoes and through the air. The cat has only one life, not nine as the proverbial legend goes, and it is our duty to make sure that it is spent in good health.

One of the first signs of a cat not feeling well is its refusal to eat. The cat can also be listless and sleepy, have red eyes and a dull coat. If it is something serious, the cat will vomit or cough and have difficulty breathing. The vet should be called immediately.

The cat's temperature should be taken with a rectal thermometer. The normal temperature range for a cat is between 100.5°F (38°C) and 102.5°F (39°C). Higher readings indicate that fever and some complication is present. If it rises above 105°F (40°C), it may be something to do with its lungs, the central nervous system, or the blood.

A low temperature is sometimes more alarming than a high one because it may indicate internal bleeding or a state of shock.

Don't become alarmed by confusing pathological facts with simple constipation or with periodical silences, which will cause the coat to become dull and the cat will tire easily. When many people suspect that a cat is not well, they will feel its temperature by touching its nose. A damp nose leads people to believe that it is healthy. Actually, the cat can have a wet nose with clear eyes even if it has a fever. A true indication of illness is when there is a drastic change in its habits, be-

The cat has an innate sense of hygiene. Getting it accustomed to using a litter box will not be difficult.

havior, and appetite: a different way of walking, resting in strange positions, excessive restlessness, and a disinterest in things that it normally likes.

Often when the cat is afflicted with a mild malady its own instincts guide it to the correct cures: spontaneous fasting, vomiting, eating grass or plants, or licking and wetting its wounds with saliva. At this time, one must attentively observe the animal and decide whether a visit to the vet is necessary.

A cat-owner should have an emergency kit on hand exclusively for the cat's needs: rectal thermometer, disinfectants, cotton, vaseline, eye-droppers, Q-tips, and other articles that a veterinarian may advise according to the age of the cat and which illnesses it tends to have.

Medicines for human use, however they've been prescribed, should never be administered to an adult cat. Do not use aspirin, tranquilizers, or prescription medications for humans on cats. A health book with vaccination dates should also be kept.

Wounds and the emergency room
It is useful to know some of the accidents that may befall a cat, which would require immediate intervention on the part of the owner or a vet.

Bite wounds: This is the most common situation whereby emergency care is needed. A dog bite especially can cause a deep and wide laceration.

The first step to take is to block the bleeding: the pressure of two fingers on a small wound may be enough; or tightly wrap the tail or limb

The cat should have several containers/bowls from which it can eat its meals.

with a bandage several times if the wound is there. Then the cat should be quickly taken to the veterinarian. In many cities, veterinarians' offices are open day and night.

If the wound doesn't appear to be serious, especially if it's small, wash it with hydrogen peroxide or warm water and soap. Don't use disinfectants because they may inflame the tissues and retard the healing process.

If the bite was inflicted by another cat or a mouse, there is the danger that an abscess will form. Bites of this kind are small, deceiving punctures and are therefore difficult to locate. It is best to immediately take the cat for an injection of antibiotics to prevent complications.

Gun wounds: These may occur in hunting areas. Also in this case, treat for shock and stop the bleeding. Try to keep the animal warm. Seek professional emergency treatment.

Trap wounds: If the cat becomes imprisoned in a trap, the wound is usually very serious, painful, and worsened by bleeding. Seek immediate professional treatment. It is often necessary to amputate part of the wounded limb.

Fish-hook wounds: These are rare but occur when cats live near rivers or lakes frequented by fishermen. The hook's barbed point should never be forcibly pulled out because it would cause major damage to the wound and the cat would do everything to try to escape. The extraction should be done by a veterinarian, who will use anesthesia, if necessary.

Along the same line, it may happen that a fish or meat bone gets

A collar may be used for an especially dear house cat. Stretchable collars are best for safety.

caught in the cat's throat. It is rare that the cat would suffocate, but it must be removed with a tweezer.

Snake bites: Swelling at the base of a very small wound can indicate a snake bite. If the snake is poisonous, the cat may begin to vomit and go into shock. The animal should be kept calm to hinder the poison from circulating through the blood; if a limb is bitten, a few inches above the wound a piece of cloth should be tied to arrest the flow of blood and keep the toxic substance from spreading. Make linear incisions over the wounds and extract the venom with a suction cup. Quickly bring the cat to the nearest veterinarian.

Burns: The natural inclination of the cat toward hot places, or through an error of estimation may cause it to burn itself on boiling pots, electric stoves, or by an actual fire. Emergency action requires applying ice or wetting the burned area with cold water and gently applying a medicinal cream. Seek professional help.

Insect bites: The cat often develops abnormal swellings to insect bites. In minor cases, it is sufficient to apply a good ointment. Pull out the stinger if one exists. In the case of a bee or wasp bite in the area of the head, or worse, in the mouth, the cat should be immediately taken to the veterinarian so as to not run the risk of asphyxia or cardiac arrest.

Automobile accidents: A cat is not capable of judging the speed at which a car is moving and, at night, may be frightened and confused by the headlights. Accidents often cause instant death. The probability of saving the cat depends on the seriousness of the wounds and how quickly it can be brought to a veterinarian. Treat for shock (keep animal

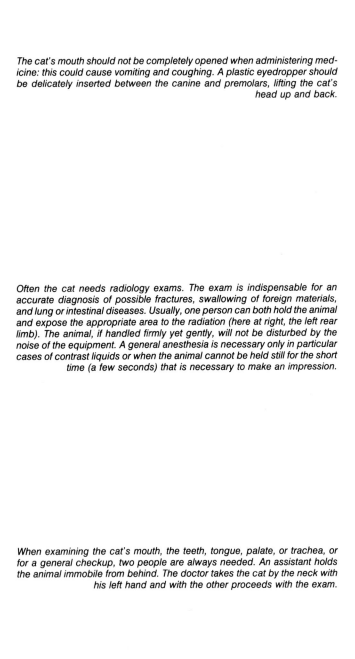

The cat's mouth should not be completely opened when administering medicine: this could cause vomiting and coughing. A plastic eyedropper should be delicately inserted between the canine and premolars, lifting the cat's head up and back.

Often the cat needs radiology exams. The exam is indispensable for an accurate diagnosis of possible fractures, swallowing of foreign materials, and lung or intestinal diseases. Usually, one person can both hold the animal and expose the appropriate area to the radiation (here at right, the left rear limb). The animal, if handled firmly yet gently, will not be disturbed by the noise of the equipment. A general anesthesia is necessary only in particular cases of contrast liquids or when the animal cannot be held still for the short time (a few seconds) that is necessary to make an impression.

When examining the cat's mouth, the teeth, tongue, palate, or trachea, or for a general checkup, two people are always needed. An assistant holds the animal immobile from behind. The doctor takes the cat by the neck with his left hand and with the other proceeds with the exam.

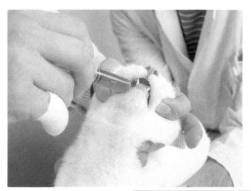

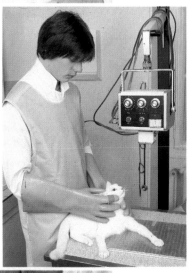

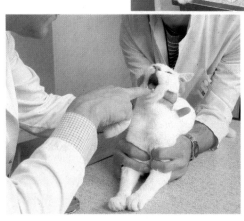

The veterinarian also needs an assistant to give injections, such as vaccinations, antibiotics, or restoratives, which are those most often administered.

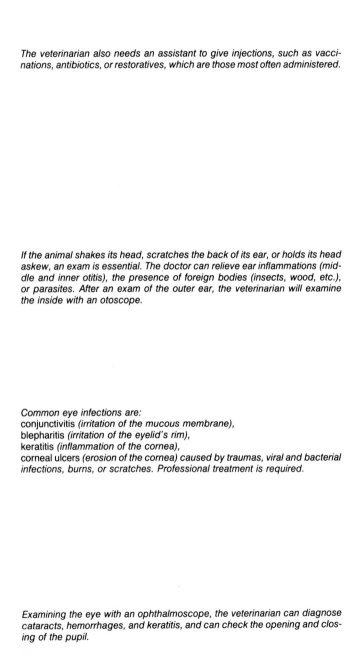

If the animal shakes its head, scratches the back of its ear, or holds its head askew, an exam is essential. The doctor can relieve ear inflammations (middle and inner otitis), the presence of foreign bodies (insects, wood, etc.), or parasites. After an exam of the outer ear, the veterinarian will examine the inside with an otoscope.

Common eye infections are:
conjunctivitis *(irritation of the mucous membrane),*
blepharitis *(irritation of the eyelid's rim),*
keratitis *(inflammation of the cornea),*
corneal ulcers *(erosion of the cornea) caused by traumas, viral and bacterial infections, burns, or scratches. Professional treatment is required.*

Examining the eye with an ophthalmoscope, the veterinarian can diagnose cataracts, hemorrhages, and keratitis, and can check the opening and closing of the pupil.

108

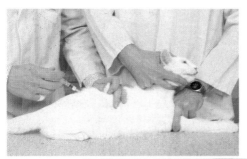

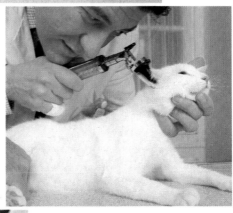

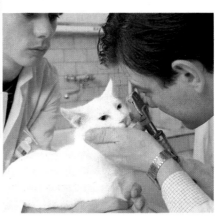

calm), stop bleeding, apply temporary splints to broken limbs, and transport the animal on a make-shift stretcher such as a board or flat surface.

The cat's defenses against heat and cold

When living out of doors, the cat learns to protect itself from the cold
and rain by taking refuge in a doorway, basement, or in an abandoned
box. The cat's fur becomes more profuse during the winter so as to
allow it to survive the low temperatures.

The house cat only occasionally risks the adventure of a night in the
wilds and with the first sign of bad weather often nestles into a warm
corner or on a cushion. It particularly likes room heaters on which it
often stretches out to sleep. However, this is not the best hygienic
position, because it dries out the coat and accelerates the shedding
process. A large object should be placed over the heater making it
impossible for the cat to rest on top.

If the cat returns home cold and with a wet coat, the cat should be
dried with a towel, especially its chest and limbs, to avoid its catching
cold that may lead to bronchitis or pneumonia.

The cat shows signs of suffering from the summer heat. It spends its
time hunting and playing, but particularly by taking long naps in the
shade of a bush or wall. In the house it will try to stretch out in a cool
part of the house where there is a breeze.

The appetite of the cat is lessened in summer, and it prefers to eat
toward evening when the sun has gone down. The strong summer sun
very much disturbs the life of a cat. If by evening its plate is still full, it
should be placed in the refrigerator or thrown away so that it doesn't go
bad overnight.

Traveling with cats

Most cats do not like to travel, but prefer to remain at home to live their
pleasant, casual existence. But the necessity may arise to go to the
veterinarian, travel on a weekend for a stay in the country, a move, or
for a mating appointment arranged between owners.

It is difficult for a cat, accustomed to a quiet life, to easily accept the
noise of traffic or a possible meeting with an unknown dog. Even if it is
held closely in someone's arms or on a leash, the cat will pull out its
nails and try to flee at the first unpleasant encounter.

A trip, long or short, should always entail the cat being placed in a
carrier designed to transport cats. It must have room to move and breath
comfortably. The cat carrier should then be placed in a well-balanced
spot in the car in case there is a sudden stop or quick turn that would
cause it to fall.

Some cats may be left free in a car, where they'll snuggle in the arms
of the passangers or in a seat or in the back. They'll remain calm until
they arrive at the destination because the owner is present. But before
putting faith into the venture, be sure that the animal is not given to
nervous conditions with sudden jumps of terror, because it may cause
an accident.

A cat should never be left alone in a car, because if it gets too hot
the cat may die of heat stroke. Nor should it be fed before leaving, as

Bandaging a wounded limb with a splint.

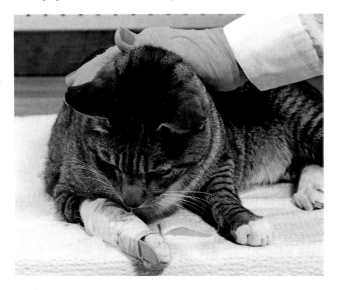

the movements of the car will not help its digestion. Upon arrival it should then be left calm for a while, possibly in the dark.

With public transportation (plane, train, bus), check first with local officials because regulations change from area to area. On planes, for example, a cat must travel in a special carrier prescribed by the airline that will be placed with the luggage. Usually the cost of a cat ticket corresponds to that of excess luggage.

Cat shows
The first cat show was held in Winchester, England, at the St. Giles Fair in 1598. But shows by modern criteria were organized almost 300 years later, by Harrison Weir at the Crystal Palace in London in 1871. This was the true beginning of cat shows and the *cat fancy* as they are defined by modern standards.

Shows in the United States became popular after one was held in 1895 at Madison Square Garden in New York City. The initiative then spread to Europe, Australia, Canada, New Zealand, South Africa, and Japan. Today, hundreds of shows take place every year all over the world. They are usually organized in the winter, inside large and well-lit showplaces, because the coats of cats with long hair are in their full splendor.

Shows in England do not last longer than a day, but in Europe and North America, they often last two days for the simple reason that long distances must be traveled by many of the participants.

Among the most important shows is the National Cat Club show held

111

in London, England, every year in December at which 2,000 pedigreed cats and another 500 non-pedigreed felines participate. In the all-important pedigree document (an English term first used for horses of pure blood and then spread to zoology and botany), the name of the animal, breed, color, sex, date of birth, and complete list of its genealogy must be stated.

In many shows there are also experimental categories open to new breeds, which do not, however, participate in championship competitions. These are in the "assessment" or "provisional class."

Subdivided into categories according to sex and age, purebred cats can earn much recognition up to Champion and the ambitious title of Grand Champion.

The Governing Council of the Cat Fancy (GCCF) is the single governing body in England that registers purebred cats, sets the standards for the breeds, and issues licenses for GCCF cat shows. This all-powerful organization sets all rules and standards for the British Cat Fancy. It became the first registering body in 1910. Since then, many British cat clubs have been formed and have subsequently been allowed to join the GCCF as affiliate members.

No omniscient body exists in the United States. The oldest cat association is the American Cat Association (ACA), formed in 1899. Other American registry associations are the American Cat Fanciers' Association (ACFA), Cat Fanciers' Federation (CFF), Crown Cat Fanciers' Federation (CCFF), United Cat Federation (UCF), The International Cat Association (TICA), and the Cat Fanciers' Association (CFA). In Canada

The cat does not like travel or water. But it knows how to adapt itself to diverse situations, as this cat which is accompanying merchants of Missouri in a painting by George Caleb Bingham.

there is the Canadian Cat Association (CCA). It must be noted that the Cat Fanciers' Association (CFA) is the largest such association in the United States, with affiliate clubs in Canada and Japan and, consequently, the most influential. It sets the standard for most of the Cat Fancy in North America.

The Cat Fancy in Europe is dominated by one of several governing bodies. The Federation Internationale Feline de l'Europe (FIFE) controls more clubs on the European continent than any of its competing associations. Its influence is felt in Austria, Belgium, Czechoslovakia, Denmark, Finland, France, Germany, Holland, Italy, Norway, Sweden, and Switzerland. Delegates from all member clubs of the various countries meet and determine the overall policies and rules of conduct. Each member club maintains their own Register of Cats and issues their own pedigree certificates.

Naturally, the cats are brought to shows in optimal condition, that is, in the best of health and with perfect coats. Most breeders own cages similar to those used in shows so as to accustom the cat to spending hours in the same cage without anxiety and to appear perfectly calm to the judges.

Grooming short-haired cats in preparation for a show is not as com-

The lazy routine at home is better than a trip anywhere. A drawing by Felix.

plicated as grooming long-haired cats. However, there is much to be done. The cat must be bathed, nails clipped, eyes and ears cleaned, tail continually inspected for grease ("stud tail"), gently brushed for removal of dead hair and, in some cases, gently combed with a pocket comb.

Preparation for showing a long-haired cat begins with kittenhood. The cat must become accustomed to hours of bathing, clipping, combing, brushing, and the many details connected with maintaining a sumptuous, long-haired coat. Every aspect of the cat's physical appearance requires devoted attention on a daily basis. Those who show their cats, long-haired or short-haired, must be dedicated groomers and health enthusiasts.

At shows in the United States, the cats are displayed in individual cages that usually measure 24 in. × 27 in. × 27 in. for a standard single cage. The standard double cage measures approximately 24 in. × 27 in. × 54 in. It is customary to decorate them with curtains, cushions, pillows, and various forms of artwork and/or fabrics. Prizes are awarded in some shows for the best-decorated cages. In addition to winning prizes exhibitors are working for points toward their cat's title of champion or grand champion.

Old age approaches slowly

If an old cat enters a new house it should be allowed sufficient freedom, left to approach the owner after it has had time for a brief, attentive study of his movements and odors. It will judge him impartially, appreciating the way in which it is fed.

A wicker basket avoids many problems when travelling with a cat.

(European) Red Marble Persian/Longhair cat proud of its trophies.

Usually, after two to three weeks of reciprocal approaches, even an old cat will be convinced that the new owner is a friend and is worth the giving and taking of affection.

But most cats eat, sleep, mate, and grow old with the same owners in the same place. A cat can live well up to the age of fifteen years, but there are many exceptions because old age may come on more quickly for cats that are stressful and poorly fed. If they've had a peaceful existence, and perhaps even if they were spayed, they live longer. But notwithstanding all of the precautions, there are healthy and happy cats that die a natural death at ten years of age, and others with uncertain health that live to twenty years of age. The oldest known living cat reached the beautiful age of thirty-seven years.

The physical decline of the cat begins at about ten years old, which is comparable to about sixty years for man. It loses its spirit, the combativeness diminishes, it sleeps longer, begins to lose some hair, gets thinner (some old cats get heavier), teeth chip or fall out, and mating doesn't interest it any longer. The eyes, however, remain shiny. Cataracts, frequent in dogs, are rare in cats.

An older cat should be taken to the vet for regular checkups. Remember that the most important precaution to keep a cat in the best of health for the longest time is to take great care in its diet.

If the cat's date of birth is not known, it isn't easy to guess the age of an old cat. It should be obvious from the condition of its teeth, but there are cases where the cat's teeth are beautiful and white even in old age. A cat's age cannot be estimated by the skin, hair, or brilliance

The jury at work.

of the eyes, because there are twelve- to fourteen-year-old cats with perfect coats and a youthful glance.

Signs of old age are more evident in females. Even if they continue to go into heat and their sexual activity is still rather active, the litters they produce are small in number and the kittens are born smaller in size. Up until about ten years old, even if they mate, often they do not become pregnant.

But at the threshold of the fatal tenth year, the weaknesses begin to appear. The hair begins to thin out, the liver and kidneys don't work to full capacity, forms of arthritis are noticed, and vascular disturbances may occur in some cats. With the new advances in veterinary science, the completeness of commercial food, and better care at home, cats are living longer and better lives.

Good-bye to the dear friend
If the house cat in its old age is stricken with an incurable disease, if it has lost the joy of eating and taking walks, if it is not enduring pain well, if it has stopped purring, it is time to perform a sad act of love. The cat has been loved very much and it has reciprocated in its own way with unmistakable affection. Now only the vet can accomplish that quick, humane gesture that liberates the cat from its suffering. For a painless euthanasia, there exist pharmaceuticals that induce immediate death.

There are cemeteries for cats and dogs if you wish to have your pet buried; associations for animal funerals also can be contacted to provide their services as well. One has the option of allowing a veterinarian to dispose of the deceased pet.

Many people who have suffered greatly at the loss of a cat swear that they'll never want another for fear of suffering the same pain again. But the offer of a friend, passing in front of a pet shop, visiting a feline show, or literature may cause one to waiver in his decision. There is always another cat that we know to be egotistical, snobby, insolent, disobedient, but extremely fascinating that is waiting to begin a new adventure of reciprocal affection with us.

Fifteen years pass in a flash, but they'll be years full of kindness, friendship, and love, which leave only unforgettable memories.

The cat's age

The following table represents the relationship of a cat's age with that of the human life span. However, it is only approximation because the breed, climate, sex, and lifestyle of each cat may alter some of the ages indicated.

CAT	HUMAN	CAT	HUMAN
1 month	5–6 months	6 years	42–44 years
2 months	9–10 months	7 years	45 years
3 months	2–3 years	8 years	48 years
4 months	5–6 years	9 years	55 years
5 months	8–9 years	10 years	60 years
6 months	14 years	11 years	62 years
7 months	15 years	12 years	65 years
8 months	16 years	13 years	68 years
1 year	18 years	14 years	72 years
2 years	25 years	15 years	74 years
3 years	30 years	16 years	76 years
4 years	35 years	17 years	78 years
5 years	38–40 years	18 years	80 years

Too many stray cats in the world

It isn't possible to state the approximate number of stray cats in the world, but an empirical estimate could suggest the existence of one stray cat for every two domestic ones. In France, there seem to be about 8 million cats of which half lead a life of wandering. In Paris, the association for the protection of animals finds about 100 to 300 cats in the streets every month. At vacation time the number increases four to five times. All large cities suffer from the same sad situation, whether with cats or dogs, abandoned by so-called owners that go away on vacation.

It is necessary to subdivide this group of abandoned cats into those completely stray, semi-stray, stray ones with an owner and home, and those domestic but occasionally stray. One of the major reasons for stray cats is the rapid proliferation of these felines caused often by owners who, rather than euthanize the litters, with false sentiments decide to abandon them in the street. The kittens, when they manage to survive, become nomads.

An adult or old cat easily adapts to a new house.

The only remedy, as is written in another section, is surgical sterilization for both males and females. Education is needed because this necessity is present at all levels of society.

The common cat becomes a breed
In the past this most available of cats had a short, striped coat and was admired by all but taken for granted as a creature of the streets and back alleys. By the end of the nineteenth century they were stabilized by caring breeders as a specific breed with many color varieties, coat patterns, and strict body type all ruled by an established standard. This cat is known as the European Shorthair, the British Shorthair, and the American Shorthair respectively, with slight differences between the three designations. Nothing offends a breeder of this established short-hair-type than to refer to them as "alley cats" or "mongrel cats." Although the majority of random-bred cats resemble the European, British, or American Shorthair, these are true purebred cats enjoying all the benefits of genetic know-how and breeder expertise.

Cross-breeds like abstract paintings
Most families have house cats that are not purebreds, which were given as gifts or taken from who knows where. They are derived from cross-breedings and their outward appearance now vaguely resembles these short-haired breeds. Sometimes they vaguely resemble breeds like the Siamese or Persian/Longhair. Of course, these cats are animals not only without pedigree, but whose mother is not even known, not to mention the fathers.

"Cats are invincible," thinks Garfield, the cat created by Jim Davis. But even a cat, sooner or later, reaches old age with all of its maladies.

A kitten is very cute at birth, perfect in its anatomical particulars and its fine coat. But as it often happens, during their growth there are many surprises: the kitten may remain very small or may assume large proportions, have a large head on a small body, small eyes positioned irregularly, short limbs, defects of temperament, and so on. A superficial example of an impurity that appears more evident as the cat grows is the coat. Because the repetition of uncontrolled cross-breeding will result in a mixture of various and unexpected colors, a litter of kittens may have nothing in common with the parents and carry the marks and stripes of previous ancestors.

Among the numerous mutations of color and design, random-bred cats are marked by mono-colored coats of black, gray-blue, taupe, striped, but often are bi-colored, tri-colored, multi-colored, in which white, black, red, and gray are mixed with the abstract imagination of a painter. To appreciate the pleasing colors and the singular disposition of the patches is to say that they are harmonious, picturesque, and beautiful.

The call of the jungle
A purebred cat, by merit of its select breeding, domestication, and closeness to humans, has become an animal with a rather well-defined character. By a quick example, it could be said that a Persian/Longhair cat is slumberous, a Siamese is restless, and a British Shorthair a good hunter of mice. But the temperament of a random-bred cat cannot be stated with any certainty since it has received various characteristics, both negative and positive, from a haphazard matching of parents.

The ideal character of a cat would be that of being cordial with people,

The different ages of the cat. Regardless of age, whether young or old, the cat quickly becomes an irreplaceable friend.

to love the house, not to scratch people or things, and not to make a mess. Most mixed-breed cats possess these good qualities with a bit of intelligence, sometimes surpassing the purebreds.

However, next to these examples of praiseworthy behavior, there are those of a capricious, independent, combative and stubborn character. If they experience shock and mistreatment, they are fearful of everything and everyone. Under such conditions domestication is very difficult, often impossible. Certain strays do not accept the minimal imposition, and they appear deaf to everything except the call to food, retreating to their obscure life as soon as possible.

Bad cats are thus predestined to a partial or full life of strayness.

Another unacceptable side of these restless cats is their tendency toward nocturnal adventures. Life becomes a matter of a cold and insecure jungle of pavement. At sunset, with the excuse that they see in the dark, they become restless and insistently meow to be let out of the house. Their real world is beyond the domestic confines where they find little animals to hunt. With mysterious mating calls they prepare themselves for sexual meetings and fights with adventurous companions that are always numerous.

Death on the pavement
A cat can often return home debased, with signs of defeat on its body and head, and it is not infrequent that certain young cats not yet accustomed to battle return with dangerous wounds. Minor lacerations do not always go away, developing into abscesses that are difficult to cure. There are many car accidents at night because drivers do not bother to

German xylograph of the fifteenth century. It is written: "Beware of cats/that lick from the front and claw from behind."

brake. Also, the piercing love calls that disturb quiet evenings are often punished by an irritated person with poisonous food when the tossing of a bit of water would be sufficient.

Contact with stray cats may cause the diffusion of some dangerous, infectious diseases like gastritis. Also scabies, due to parasitic mites that penetrate layers under the skin, is a frequent infection with stray cats.

The quiet nocturnal revelry is over at dawn. But not all cats return to the fold, because they're not satiated. During the period of mating they prefer to wander more and perhaps continue for a week or longer, when at the end of their strength they appear at the kitchen seeking a dish of food.

The semi-stray cats with owners prefer not to go too far from home, while true stray ones—the orphans—choose to live in the areas of old warehouses with accessible basements. They furnish comfortable refuge where the cats may hunt among the garbage and find sad remains on which to feed itself. As always, mice will be the most desirable find.

If during the day the neighborhood is too noisy and full of commotion and people, dogs, and cars appear as enemies, and the cats will remain in hiding, renouncing even the hunt for food. Some cats, however, will risk going out to stretch themselves out in the sun. They may remain also under a window where they know some friend will sooner or later toss them a bit of food.

When a stray cat is sick or wounded, it attempts to cure itself. It will

Group of kittens (above) and two male adults at the beginning of a duel (below), belonging to a colony of stray cats.

Domestic cat (above) and ferel cat (opposite).

go to a quiet spot and use its saliva as a good ointment for all ills. But for infectious illnesses, neither saliva nor individual resilience will help. There is a small consolation: infectious diseases limit the number of street cats with a natural decimation. If a sudden drop in the feline population of a neighborhood is observed, it is a sign that some epidemic has cut down a large quantity of these legendary vagabonds.

When their end is at hand, cats try to find a secluded spot in which to die with dignity—either under a bush, in the trunk of a tree, or a crumbled hut so as not to disturb or be disturbed in the moment of the most quiet sleep.

Millions of stray cats, lost cats, and abandoned cats in Britain and the United States are rounded up each year by local animal wardens and animal welfare societies, and disposed of in various ways. Although these unfortunate cats are made available for adoption by kind and sensitive humans, the large majority are euthanized in an excessive expenditure of life. Through a massive education program extolling the benefits of neutering and responsible, humane attitudes, it is hoped that this condition will eventually change.

Understanding your cat
If the contract between humans and cats is to be honored, then it is necessary for humans to grasp the unique nature of feline behavior. The domestic cat, unlike the domestic dog, lives with its wild instincts always

WHAT HAVE I DONE TO
DESERVE ALL THESE KITTENS.

The cat is one of the American cartoonist George Herriman's favorite subjects.

close to the surface. If allowed, it will close the door to domesticity forever, leaving the hurt human with a painful mystery. From the sacred tombs of Egypt to the suburbs of Britian and America, it is quite possible for the *Felis domestica* to return to the wild and roaming life with all its dangers and intrigues. This can only happen when cat-lovers, in well-intended ignorance, treat their cats like dogs, children, or stuffed animals. Although many of the cats confined in animal pounds have been abandoned, a great number of them have simply run away, creating many homeless kittens in their free-roaming state. Cats that are treated like cats tend to remain happily in their domestic situation.

Cats are born to be solitary creatures in the wild, claiming territory, mating, and hunting for a living. They were never really intended to live the life of a pet. With the exception of lions, cats in the wild spend most of their time in quiet solitude, coming together only to mate or rear cubs. All cats, even your mild-mannered kitty, would live that lifestyle without the intervention of sensitive humans with their offers of generosity and admiration.

The reason cats deny their wild instincts and accept the social contract between themselves and their human caretakers is not difficult to understand. Firstly, cats of today are the progeny of hundreds of generations of cats before them who have accepted domesticity. By the weight of sheer genetic influence, domesticity has evolved a more home-like companion animal than those who formerly roamed the jungles, plains, and mountains of the world. Consequently, living in a house is a pleasant idea worth considering to the domestic cat just entering a new home. Secondly, human intervention comes at a very critical period in the development of the average house cat's life. By taking responsibility for the cat's food, litter box, warmth, amusement, and feelings of security in kittenhood, we interfere with their process of maturity in preparation for a life in the wild. In a sense, domestic cats are adolescents who never grow up completely, never look beyond the horizon of their immediate circumstances, and never leave home.

However, it is necessary to satisfy those few instincts that can never be altered by the whir of the electric can-opener. If your cat hunts mice it must be allowed to do that. Unless the male or female is surgically altered (sexually neutered) it must be allowed to mate. Spaying or castrating is most consistent with the domestic lifestyle of a pet. House cats need to be left alone when they so desire just as they need companionship and affection when they ask for it. Anything short of these conditions is to create an unworkable situation for both humans and cats.

Living with a cat is a rare opportunity to bring a bit of untamed nature into your life. Cats have much to teach us with their uninhibited manner and strong sense of personal identity. Cats know who they are and appear to be quite pleased with themselves. Is it instinct or a healthy sense of ego? You must decide for yourself.

The breed descriptions in this book were meant to introduce the reader to the great variety of coat colors, patterns, and types as well as body types and characteristics. They delineate the physical cat from breed to breed, helping the reader to form a mental portrait. These breed descriptions are not the official standards of the Cat Fanciers Association, Inc., of the United States (CFA) or the Governing Council of the Cat Fancy of Great Britian (GCCF). However, in many respects they conform to the North American standards, differing in some points of detail from British standards.

Odd-eyed White Persian/Longhair

1   BALINESE

Origin   In the 1950s, in America, litters of Siamese cats were born with mutant kittens among them. Instead of having the traditional short hair of the breed, the kittens had long, silky hair. They became the first of a new breed, a breed initially called the Long-haired Siamese. But breeders of traditional short-haired Siamese challenged the new breed, and thus it came to be called Balinese, in spite of the fact that the island of Bali had nothing at all to do with the matter.

Coat   Long, silky, without undercoat and also without the collar characteristic of other long-haired breeds.

Color   Colorpoint is the contrasting color pattern of a lighter coat with darker points (face mask, ears, legs, feet, and tail).

Seal Point: May range from light tawny to cream coat, paler on the belly and chest. The face is completely covered by a dark brown mask except for the forehead, merging into light lines at the ears. Dark brown ears, tail, and paws with the mask make up the points.

Blue Point: Ice-white coat with dark blue markings.

Chocolate Point: Ivory coat with chocolate markings.

Lilac Point: Ice-white coat with rose-gray markings.

Body   Long and light with good muscling. Its movements are nimble and graceful, reminiscent of the movements of Balinese dancers. Slender legs, with the hind legs longer than the forelegs.

Head   Wedge-shaped, well-proportioned head on a slender neck. The ears are broad at the base, the nose is long and straight.

Eyes   Deep blue, almond-shaped.

Tail   Long, tapering.

Character   Sociable, affectionate, intelligent, the Balinese is acrobatic in its leaps. The voice is imploring, of approximately the same tone and strength of the voice of its cousin the Siamese.

Ideal owner   Shows affection toward all members of the family, but gives itself most openly to one person.

Environment   A good apartment cat that still is fond of open spaces on the terrace and in the garden.

Diet   A strong, healthy animal, not choosy in its diet.

Care   Brushing and combing as for all long-haired breeds. The coat is less likely to get knots than the Persian.

Reproduction   Each litter counts three or four kittens. If a Balinese is crossed with a Siamese, the kittens have the characteristics of the Siamese but with a feltlike, short coat. Balinese mature sexually earlier than any other long-haired breed. They are fine parents and play a great deal with their young.

Faults   Eye color other than blue, crossed eyes, albino nose, weak hind legs, presence of undercoat, tail not meeting standard, sickly nature.

Varieties   Balinese cats in all the other colors found in Colorpoint Shorthairs are called Javanese. (See Javanese.) As the Balinese is a long-haired Siamese, the Javanese is a long-haired Colorpoint Shorthair.

Top: Seal Point
Bottom: Blue Point

2 BIRMAN
Sacred Cat of Burma

Origin The breed's origins are lost in legend. The first specimens probably lived in Burma, in the golden age of Lao-Tsun, protected by the Grand Lama of the Buddhists. Together with other cats, the Birman was venerated as a divinity and, like the others, held to be an oracle. The Persian/Longhair component supplied the long, silky coat now characteristic of the Birman.

Coat Long or fairly long, thick on the neck and tail, silky, well distributed on the back and flanks, lightly wavy on the belly. The hair is shorter on the muzzle but thickens on the cheeks. The coat never becomes matted or rough.

Color There are several varieties of Birman, which all share the characteristic of pure white gloves on all four feet. A quality Birman must have this important marking.

Seal Point: Golden cream coat, white gloves, blue eyes; mask, ears, tail, and paws are dark seal brown.

Blue Point: Similar to the Seal Point, but with gray-blue mask, ears, tail, and paws.

Lilac Point: Mask, ears, tail, and paws are pearl gray.

Chocolate Point: Mask, ears, tail, and paws are chestnut brown.

An American variety of short-haired Birman is known as Snowshoe Cat because of the white gloves. This variant is recognized by only a few small clubs and has not yet attained any notable popularity. (Please see the Snowshoe section.)

Body Long, massive body supported on medium-length strong legs, well-proportioned frame, short, strong paws.

Head Round, broad, with strong bones. Straight nose, broad cheeks, strong mouth, thick whiskers. When seen in profile, the ears look slanted.

Eyes Slightly slanted, very beautiful deep, brilliant blue. Expression of the eyes described as "fascinating."

Tail Robust, well feathered.

Character Unique because of its strange manner of movement, coat, and mysterious eyes. Although related to the Siamese, it has a tranquil nature, sociable at play. Faithful and intelligent, it speaks in a sweet, well-behaved voice.

Ideal owner The Birman loves the family and is outgoing toward persons who share certain of its own characteristics, including tranquility. It silently offers its entire devotion to the family, but when its owner is away the cat tends toward distraction and indifference.

Environment A good apartment cat, but in nice weather it likes to go for walks on the terrace or in the garden.

Diet The Birman has a measured appetite, preferring meat over other foods.

Care Regular brushing and combing are necessary.

Reproduction Kittens are born with a light-colored, solid coat. The dark markings appear after a few months. The female is willing to mate frequently and with fervor.

Faults Defective gloves, crossed or badly colored eyes, pointed muzzle, dark coat, kinked or otherwise deformed tail.

Top: Lilac Point
Bottom: Seal Point

3 CYMRIC

Origin This long-haired Manx began showing up in litters of normal short-haired Manx in Canada in the 1960s. Because these cats appeared in carefully pedigreed litters, the record contends there were no Persian/Longhair crosses to create such a long coat. The long-haired cats were carefully bred together and bred true, giving us the Cymric. Because the Isle of Man (origin of the Manx) is in the Irish Sea halfway between Ireland and Wales, these Manx cousins were given the Celtic name for Welsh, Cymric (pronounced Kim'rik).

Coat The coat is medium to long in length, with a thick undercoat but is different from the Persian/Longhair. The Cymric coat is more of medium length and easily groomed; it seldom mats. The top hairs are shiny and smooth.

Color All colors and combinations are accepted. (All other features of the Cymric are exactly like the Manx.)

Top: Tortoiseshell
Bottom: Brown Tabby

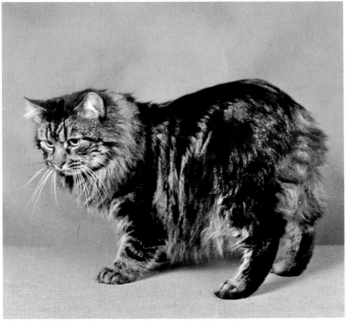

Origin First produced in 1924 by crossings among Siamese, Birman, and Persian/Longhair cats. In Britain they are considered to be Persians/Longhairs in other colors rather than a separate breed. The name Himalayan comes from the Himalayan rabbit, similar in color to the cat.

Coat One might say that the Himalayan/Colorpoint Longhair is a Persian/Longhair in Siamese colors. The Himalayan/Colorpoint Longhair's coat is about 4.75 in. (12 cm.) long, thick, silky, resilient, with an abundant ruff.

Color Various colors are recognized.

Seal Point: Golden cream coat with seal brown mask, ears, legs, feet, and tail.

Blue Point: White coat with blue mask, legs, and tail.

Chocolate Point: Ivory-white coat with strong chocolate markings.

Lilac Point: Magnolia-white coat with lilac markings.

Red Point: Pale white coat with red markings.

Tortie Point: Cream coat with tortoiseshell markings.

Blue-Cream Point: Blue-white coat with blue points mottled with patches of cream.

Lynx Point: Markings are Tabby design in variety of colors.

As with the Siamese, all varieties must have well-marked mask, ears, legs, paws, and tail.

Body Solid, over strong legs. It reaches perfection at eighteen months old.

Head Broad, rounded, in typical Persian/Longhair style, with plump cheeks, short nose, small and wide-set ears, short neck, very long whiskers.

Eyes Round, broad, of a lovely sapphire blue.

Tail Straight, not thickly haired, with no kinkiness.

Character Affectionate, good-natured, playful, gentle, forgiving, does not fight with other cats, rarely shows the capriciousness of its Siamese forebears. An exceptional mouser, quick to learn. Pleasant and musical voice.

Ideal owner This breed quickly becomes fond of the whole family, but perhaps its sweetness of character has best prepared it to live with one person.

Environment Cats of this breed have adapted well to apartment life, but they do like a bit of space.

Diet Meat with a little rice and vegetables.

Care Regular combing.

Reproduction Males are sexually mature at eighteen months old, considerably later than females. Each litter is of two or three kittens, but it is difficult to obtain perfect specimens. The young are born with short hair, entirely white, and only at six months old are the markings established.

Faults Long, triangular Siamese head; frail bone structure; crossed eyes or of any other color but blue; short hair; spots not specified in standard.

Varieties Some solid-colored kittens are born in Himalayan/Colorpoint Longhair litters, either chocolate or lilac. They are given separate breed status—Kashmirs—by some organizations in America, considered Himalayans by others. The British consider them Persians/Longhairs.

Top: Seal Point
Bottom: Tortie Point

5 JAVANESE

Origin When Balinese cats were first bred from mutant Siamese long-haired kittens, they were perfected in the basic Siamese colors: Seal Point, Blue Point, Chocolate Point, and Lilac Point. The breeding programs have expanded gradually to include a wide range of colorpoints comparable to the Colorpoint Shorthair. (The Colorpoint Shorthair is the Siamese cat in other colors.) So one might describe the Javanese as a Colorpoint Shorthair with long hair or a Balinese in other Siamese coat colors. It is a Siamese cat with long fur in a wide variety of colors.

Coat Long, silky, without undercoat and without the collar characteristic of other long-haired breeds.

Color

Red Point: Cream body with orange-red markings.

Cream Point: Cream body with buff markings.

Tortie Point: Tawny body with red and cream patched markings.

Blue-Cream Point: White body with blue and cream patched markings.

Lilac-Cream Point: Glacial white body with pinkish gray and cream patched markings.

All of the above colors can come in the Lynx Point design, which is Tabby markings on the points. For instance, one might see a Red Lynx Point Javanese.

(All other characteristics are the same as the Balinese.)

Top and bottom: Red Point

6 KASHMIR

Origin These solid-colored Himalayans/Colorpoint Longhairs are the subject of much disagreement. They were born in litters of Himalayans/Colorpoint Longhairs and have been bred to each other to create pure coats with rich colors of chocolate or lilac (which is really a pale version of chocolate). The British consider the Himalayan/Colorpoint Longhair a form of the Persian/Longhair, so Kashmirs are also considered Persians/Longhairs in Great Britain. Some organizations in America consider them to be solid-color Himalayans, while others feel that all Himalayans must have colorpoints. But whatever the classification, Kashmirs are beautiful, Persian/Longhair-type cats with long chocolate or lilac solid-colored coats.

(All other characteristics are the same as the Himalayan/Colorpoint Longhair.)

Top and bottom: Chocolate

7 MAINE COON CAT

Origin The origins of the breed are obscure, but it is thought that it must have been developed in Maine by crossing American house cats with Angoras. The Maine Coon was greatly admired in shows a century ago, until the arrival on the scene of the Persians/Longhairs diminished its popularity.

Coat Short on the head, beginning to lengthen on the withers and thicken greatly on the body and tail. The fur is soft and silky, but less luxurious than the coat of the Persian/Longhair. An original characteristic of the coat is its similarity to that of the raccoon. A popular tradition holds that the Maine Coon is actually descended from the raccoon, but such a cross between a domestic cat and the wild raccoon is genetically impossible.

Color The standard allows twenty-five different colors, both solid and mixed, plus eight Tabby combinations, which are divided into four groups: solid, tabby, tabby and white, others.

Body This large breed is muscular, handsome, and so regular in form that the silhouette can be inscribed in a rectangle.

Head Big, rounded, with medium neck. The ears are tufted and carried erect.

Eyes Large, oval, yellowish or of a color harmonizing with the color of the coat (green, gold, copper). Only white Maine Coons can have blue eyes.

Tail Thickly feathered, of medium length, ending in a substantial tuft of hair.

Character The Maine Coon is intelligent, shrewd, affectionate, home-loving, and a great mouser and hunter of other small animals.

Ideal owner The Maine Coon is friendly toward the entire family, but selects one person to whom it gives itself entirely.

Environment This cat prefers a garden to wander in, but it is a good apartment cat, especially when altered.

Diet Meat and fish, alternately. (The Coon was often a sailor's cat in the past.)

Care Should be combed like an Angora or Persian/Longhair. It is a healthy cat, capable of withstanding even cold climates.

Reproduction The normal litter is two or three kittens, and the young may be quite different from one another. They develop slowly and reach full maturity only at four years old.

Faults Scanty coat, flaccid musculature.

Top: Black and White
Bottom: Brown Tabby and White

8 NORWEGIAN FOREST CAT
Norsk Skaukatt

Origin Records of this cat from cold northern climates date from antiquity. The breed is mentioned in Norwegian mythology and reappears in a dominant role in the Nordic fables written between 1837 and 1852, where it is described as an enchanted cat with a long, thick tail. This single Scandinavian breed was recognized in 1930; it was shown in Oslo before World War II.

Coat Heavy and thick, offering great protection against the cold. The woolly undercoat keeps the body warm, while the medium hair protects the animal from rain and snow. This cat has an abundant ruff.

Color All colors are permitted.

Body Robust, muscular, with powerful legs. Its extraordinary claws make it possible for the cat to climb rocks as well as trees.

Head Round and strong.

Eyes Bright and attentive. The colors vary with the color of the coat.

Tail Of medium length, thickly furred.

Character Necessity has made this breed cautious, intelligent, swift, and a fine hunter.

Ideal owner The Forest Cat likes human company.

Environment An independent cat that likes open spaces, it also accepts life in a house offering it a certain freedom.

Diet Meat and fish. The Forest Cat often provides its own food by hunting.

Care It should be combed only occasionally. Like all cats, it sheds once a year, when only the tail reminds us that it is a long-haired cat.

Brown Tabby

9 PERSIAN/LONGHAIR

Origin There were no long-haired cats in Europe before 1500. Evidence is found in documents from 1520 of the Angora, which is Turkish in origin. The Persian/Longhair is descended from the Angora, but it is considered a modern breed, since scientific selective breeding began only in 1871.

It seems certain that the first Persian/Longhair was taken to Italy in the eighteenth century by the explorer Pietro della Valle, who was fond of these very beautiful cats with their long, dense coat, never before seen in the western world. A century later, although jealously guarded by Italian fanciers, the breed was taken to France and England, where it was refined by cross-breeding with the Angora, giving it a silkier coat and broadening the variety of colors.

In Britain and Europe the Persians are simply called Longhairs; each color is considered a separate breed and thought to have slightly different characteristics because of the different cross-breeding done to attain their colors. In America they are all Persians of different colors.

The numerous enthusiasts of Persians/Longhairs today claim that their favorite has everything: the long hair, so pleasant to the touch when petted, the grace of its every movement, the most luminous and profound expression of the eyes imaginable, noble beauty.

Coat Abundant, thick, resilient, loose-fitting on the body, denser on the neck and shoulders, where it forms a leonine mane, well-furred legs. The long hair is typical of domestic felines. Indeed, wild felines with long hair do not exist, with the exception of the snow leopard and the North American lynx, both of which grow longer hair in winter.

Color Persians/Longhairs are separated into three divisions of colors: (1) solid colors, black, white, blue, cream, reddish [russet], with orange eyes; (2) more than one color, with eye color varying with coat color, chinchilla, white ground with black flecks on the back, tail, and head; black smoke (white hair with black tips); black-yellow (tortoiseshell) and black-yellow-white; (3) various colors and patterns, from gray to brown, from blue to orange; tiger (resembling the markings of the tiger); marbled, (patterns similar to variegated marble).

Black: The color must be glossy black, compact to the roots, uniform, without patterns or light hairs or any other coloring. They should be kept out of the sun to avoid alteration of the color toward brown. Breeding of the black variety is difficult, and kittens do not attain the best color until six or seven months old. It is an extraordinarily beautiful cat, passionate and affectionate to its owners. The eyes are big—deep orange or copper.

White with blue eyes: This variety recalls its relation to the Angora. It is the only type with blue eyes. Unfortunately, many of these are deaf from birth. Nature has compensated for this defect by granting them a particular sensitivity and an attentive capability, which make up for their deafness. A classical salon cat, tranquil, affectionate, extremely clean.

Top: Black
Bottom: White (orange eyes)

To keep the coat clean: an occasional bath; complete brushings with talcum or dry shampoo.

White with orange eyes: This variety is the result of a cross between Blue and Cream Persians/Longhairs. It has a stocky body, short legs, round head with orange or copper eyes, and a pure white coat with no suggestion of other shades. It should be given the same care as its blue-eyed cousin. This variety is not deaf, which suggests that deafness is somehow associated genetically with blue eyes. There is also a White one with one blue and one orange eye.

Blue: This is perhaps the most precious variety; it is superbly bred in Britain. The coat is silky, extremely long, lavender-blue. The eyes are big and round, either deep orange or copper. Majestic gait and gentle in character.

Cream: The result of careful cross-breeding between White and Red Persians/Longhairs, the Cream variety has a coat that varies from intense ivory to yellow or pale tawny, without shadows, with either orange or copper eyes. The males are invariably more attractive than the females, which are also not good breeders. Care as for White ones: frequent baths will improve the coat more than daily brushing. Good temperament, playful, sweet-natured, affectionate.

Red: This variety is rare because it is difficult to produce. Often the color of the coat is imperfect. The standard calls

Below: Blue
Opposite top: Red
Opposite bottom: Cream

for red-orange hair, uniform without streaking, and copper eyes.

The Persian/Longhair Tabby can be seen in three patterns: Classic Tabby, Mackerel Tabby, or Patched Tabby. (Please see American Shorthair Tabby for full description.)

Brown Tabby: The base color of the coat is sand brown, with tawny tones and marbling formed by streaking in the form of black bands, which is reminiscent of wild felines. The orange eyes stand out clearly from the dark coat. This variety is produced only with difficulty because of the complicated patterns required by the standard. The Brown Tabby should be brushed often to eliminate knots in the hair. It is sociable and gentle but is also a good mouser.

Silver Tabby: This is a rare variety because it is hard to produce in its full beauty. The color must be pale silver with distinct black stripes on the head, two rings on the neck, dark rings on legs and tail, butterfly patterns on the shoulders, and oystershell patterns on the flanks. The eyes are luminous green or hazel. This variety is robust, healthy, clean, affectionate, intelligent, and a fine hunter.

Red Tabby: A splendid, fascinating variety with a bright red coat setting off darker coloring on head, cheeks, chest, and legs. The tail is strong and flowing, the same color as the coat to the tip. The eyes are big and round, orange or copper in color. Breeding is difficult because defective specimens are frequent, with such faults as a narrow muzzle or faint markings on the coat. In North America the Cameo Tabby is also bred. It has a cream coat with Red Tabby markings, whereas the Red Tabby has a red coat with dark red markings.

Also found in America:

Blue Tabby: Ivory coat with blue-gray markings.

Cream Tabby: Cream coat with buff markings.

Brown Patched Tabby: Coppery brown coat with black markings and patches of red and/or cream.

Blue Patched Tabby: Ivory coat with deep blue markings and cream patches.

Silver Patched Tabby: Silver coat with black markings and red and/or cream patches.

All of the above have copper eyes.

Chinchilla: This variety is descended from the Silver Tabby. It must have a snowy white coat, finely specked with black on the back, flanks, head, ears, and tail. The green eyes have a dark border that seems to be penciled on. The Chinchilla achieves the maximum of elegance and fascination. Curiously, the kittens are born with dark streaking which grows fainter and finally disappears as the cat grows. This type is very playful and affectionate and requires gentle humans as owners. It is an ideal cat for someone living alone.

Shaded Silver: The coat seems to have silver in it and, although darker, in some ways resembles the Chinchilla. It has a delicate and seductive beauty. The eyes are green rimmed with black. Not well known in Europe, it has attained popularity in America and Canada. In Britain this variety is called Pewter and has orange eyes with a black rim.

Top: Brown Tabby
Bottom: Red Tabby

Chinchilla, Shaded, and Shell Varieties: These luxurious cats all refer to different degrees of tipped color over white or cream undercoats. They are particularly popular in North America.

Shaded and Shell Cameo: White undercoat with red tipping and copper eyes.

Shaded and Chinchilla Golden: Golden undercoat with brown tipping and green eyes.

Shaded and Shell Tortoiseshell: Tortoiseshell tipping, which means that the long hairs appear to be brushed in black with patches of red and cream, copper eyes.

Smoke: The coat is black with silver highlights on the sides and flanks, with white undercoat and black feet. The coat is very dense with an abundant ruff. The expression of the orange or copper eyes is sweet. Breeding is difficult. This is an extremely handsome cat, daring, intelligent, strong, and affectionate toward the family. Attentive care of the coat is necessary.

North Americans also breed:

Blue Smoke: Blue with white undercoat, copper eyes.

Cameo Red: Red with white undercoat, copper eyes.

Smoke Tortoiseshell: Black with white undercoat and red and cream patches, copper eyes.

Tortoiseshell: Black, red, and cream are distinct colors on this handsome Persian. The colors should be distinct and glossy for a true tortoiseshell. The eyes are orange or copper and very expressive. The kittens are usually females, and the rare males are sterile; female Tortoiseshells must be mated with Black, Red, or Cream Persian/Longhair males for this reason. They make excellent mother cats and are delightful company in the home.

Tortoiseshell with white: Colors include black, red, and cream uniformly distributed and separated by white. All kittens are females, and the variety is closely related to the Tortoiseshell described above. For breeding, they must be mated with bi-colored males.

Blue-Cream: This variety normally results from mating the male Cream with the female Blue. The silky coat is thus bicolor blue and cream, delicately blended in such a way that neither color predominates. The eyes are orange or dark copper. Only the females can be bred, since males are sterile. The Blue-Cream has an extremely sweet temperament and is particularly adapted to life with one person, from whom it demands attentive care.

Peke-Face Red: Derived from the Red Persian/Longhair, this variety has a face resembling that of the Pekingese dog, with a short nose and a depression between the eyes. There is also a Peke-Face Red Tabby.

Calico: Where the Tortoiseshell is black with patches of white and red, the Calico is white with patches of black and red.

Dilute Calico: White with patches of blue and cream. The eyes are copper on both types of Calico.

Bi-Color: This cat can be black and white, blue and white, red and white, or cream and white. It must have white feet,

Top: Tortoiseshell and White (Calico)
Bottom: Chinchilla

legs, undersides, chest, and muzzle; it should have an inverted "V" in the colors on its face. The Persian Van Bi-Color is white with the same colors confined to the head, tail, and legs. The eyes are copper.

Body   According to the general provisions of the standard, the body can be from 16 to 20 in. (40 to 50 cm.) long, preferably on the long side, with the tail measuring from 10 to 12 in. (25 to 30 cm.) in length. Height at the shoulder is about 12 in. (30 cm.). All Persians/Longhairs must have a massive body with strong musculature on a sturdy skeleton. The "setting" of the body is even more important than the majesty of the coat. The legs should be short and muscular with large feet.

Head   Broad, round, massive, without angularities; plump cheeks. The neck is strong, the ears small and widely spaced with a graceful tuft. The jaws are strong, the nose short and saddled.

Eyes   Ample, round, shining, expressive, and of well-defined color harmonizing with the dominant color of the coat.

Tail   Magnificently supplied with hair, ending in a plume that is carried low to the ground. The tail is one of the distinctive attributes of all Persians.

Character   Generally speaking, only calm is apparent, concealing a strong temperament together with a great desire for affection. It combines traits of likeableness, sweetness, gaiety, sociability (even toward other cats), and fidelity. It has an aristocratic bearing. Some varieties are enthusiastic mousers. The Persian/Longhair rarely shows its claws.

Ideal owner   Exceptionally affectionate toward its owners and their friends who are good with cats.

Environment   It is the classic apartment cat.

Diet   Balanced and varied. Some specimens, if fat and overfed, may have cardiac complications. The ideal daily diet is ¼ lb. (100 g) of meat (or fish, lung, or spleen) balanced by a bit of rice and cooked vegetables supplemented, especially in the first year, by multiple-vitamin drops. Persians normally tolerate milk.

Care   Swallowing hairs can cause intestinal and respiratory problems. Therefore, the rich coat must have daily intensive brushing with a soft natural-bristle brush (metal brushes can break the hairs), with particular attention to the tail, which is often the target of fleas. To ensure the full splendor of the Persian/Longhair coat, use dry shampoo. If the cat is very dirty, it should be washed in lukewarm water with a neutral soap, then immediately rinsed and dried. In kittens the longer hair begins to grow in around the seventh week of life. Careful brushing may begin at this point.

Reproduction   Maternity may cause problems in some varieties since the two or three kittens in each litter can be delicate at birth and need constant attention until the fourth month. The mother should be carefully cared for during pregnancy and after delivery, including vitamin and calcium supplements. It is wise to avoid in-breeding. Blue Persian/Longhair females bred to their fathers or brothers can miscarry or give birth to defective kittens.

Faults   Insufficient hair, elongated muzzle, leanness, difference in coloring of tail from coat, close-set ears.

Top: Blue-Cream
Bottom: Shell Cameo

Origin According to a popular legend, this breed was created with a female White Persian/Longhair who was injured in an automobile accident, which resulted in the cat's being unable to feel pain or face up to dangers. Geneticists give little credence to the belief and insist that the cat's docile temperament is the result of frequent selective breeding among domestic cats. The breed is still considered controversial. They can be found in America.

Coat Long or semi-long, rather heavy.

Color The standard recognizes colorpoints (Chocolate, Seal, Lilac, and Blue) in contrast to a lighter coat with or without white mittens, as found in the Birman. Sometimes Parti-colors and Bi-colors are recognized.

Body Soft in structure. When picked up, the cat gives the impression of being a bundle of rags, hence its name.

Head Tending to roundness with broad cheeks and a short nose.

Eyes Slanted, blue.

Tail Robust and well furred.

Character Extremely mild.

Ideal owner The cat gets along best with tranquil owners.

Environment It is happiest when living almost exclusively in an apartment.

Diet Meat with vegetables and rice.

Care Combing and brushing with the hands or light implements.

Faults Crossed eyes, long muzzle, deformations in the tail.

Top and bottom: Seal Point

Origin   The Somali was bred in America from mutant Abyssinian Longhairs in the late 1960s. The long-haired gene is believed to have been introduced in the Abyssinian from a Persian around 1900.

Coat   It has soft, double-coated fur of medium length. Those with a dense coat, ear tufts, and a thick collar are especially prized.

Color   Similar to the Abyssinian, Somalis can be Ruddy (orange-brown tipped with black) or Red (red tipped with brown).

Body   Elongated, sturdy but graceful, a little larger than the Abyssinian. Strong, slender legs. A slightly arched back, which gives the impression that the animal is ready to perform a jump.

Head   Round, tapering into an elongated muzzle, aristocratic. Wide ears, always alert.

Eyes   Green or golden, rich in color, surrounded by a dark lidskin as if they were outlined with dark pencil. Slightly almond-shaped, they are deep, expressive, with a charming gaze.

Tail   Long, strong, thickly haired.

Character   It has a wild appearance, but in reality it is a tame cat, even if sometimes mistrustful. It is very lively, intelligent, shrewd, a good mouser and hunter of small game.

Ideal owner   It is an animal that wants to be certain of the trust and respect of its owner before giving itself completely.

Environment   Lives indoors willingly, but it has an absolute necessity to be free at least on a large terrace or in a garden when the weather is good.

Diet   It is a glutton for meat and giblets.

Care   It fears the cold; in winter it is necessary to create a temperate climate for it.

Reproduction   Two or three very small and dark kittens are born in a litter. The color and the long hair develop at about eighteen months old.

Faults   Small size, insufficient fur, excessive shyness.

Top: Red (sorrel) and Ruddy (usual)—kittens
Bottom: Ruddy (usual)

Origin   The Tiffany is a Burmese cat with long hair. It was bred in North America and retains the Burmese seal brown color.

Coat   A long, silky coat that develops rather late in the kitten.

Color   A deep seal brown is even throughout the coat.

(All the other characteristics are the same as the Burmese.)

Seal Brown

13   TURKISH ANGORA

Origin   Angoras are of Turkish origin and the progenitors of the Persian/Longhair breed. Long-haired cats were known as Angoras for decades because the earliest ones came from the Turkish city of Angora (Ankara), the region also known for a goat with extremely soft hair known as mohair. Asia Minor is also known to be particularly favorable to the growth of animal hair. The true Angora is a breed that was slowly becoming extinct as it was replaced by the Persian/Longhair. However, the breed is being revived in the United States with cats imported from the Ankara Zoo. Great Britain does not yet recognize the Turkish Angora nor does America recognize the Turkish Van.

Coat   Soft, fine, and silky, the fur is thick on the neck, belly, and tail. Shedding in summer is so evident that the Angora almost looks like a short-haired cat. But in winter the coat becomes thick very rapidly. There is no undercoat as in the Persian/Longhair, and for this reason brushing the Angora is much easier.

Color   Once the only true Angora was white, and even today it is the preferred color. Black, Blue, Black Smoke, Blue Smoke, Silver Tabby, Red Tabby, Brown Tabby, Blue Tabby, Calico, and Bi-color are now accepted varieties. (See American Shorthair for description.)

Body   Robust, slightly longer than the Persian/Longhair, the Angora is graceful in its movements. Of delicate bone structure, the Angora seems bigger than it actually is because of its luxurious coat.

Head   Medium size, tapering toward the chin. Large, pointed ears with ear tufts. Delicate, beautiful neck.

Eyes   The first Angoras brought from Turkey had blue, almond-shaped eyes or one blue and one orange eye. Today, blue and amber eyes are acceptable, and other colors are tolerated. White Angoras with blue eyes may be born deaf.

Tail   Long, well plumed, tapered. Sometimes when the cat is in motion the tail is carried over the back, almost touching the head.

Character   The Angora is a well-behaved cat, sweet and affectionate by nature, very intelligent. Its constant immobility gives the Angora a sphinxlike appearance.

Ideal owner   The Angora prefers to live with one person who is disposed to admiration, love and respect for its serenity.

Environment   Totally a house cat.

Diet   The preferred food is meat, but the cat is not finicky.

Care   The Angora should be brushed and combed daily. Cats living in cities usually have dirty coats. Since they do not like water, like the Turkish Van, they should be cleaned regularly with dry shampoo.

Reproduction   The kittens are precocious. They are active and play very early, but they do not develop the Angora coat until two years old. The Ankara Zoo has been working in recent years on preservation of this Turkish national cat.

Faults   Short hair, wavy coat, spotting, short tail.

Top and bottom: White

Origin   This Angora cat had its remote origin in the snowy region of Lake Van in Turkey. It was brought to England in 1955, and it was officially recognized in 1969. England does not recognize the Turkish Angora yet, and America does not yet recognize the Turkish Van.

Coat   As a defense against the bitter cold of its native habitat, the Turkish Van has a soft, silky, and dense coat, but with no woolly undercoat. In winter its coat may rival that of the Persian/Longhair, while in summer it is greatly thinned.

Color   The base color is white, without yellowish traces. Chestnut-red markings should be present near the ears. The tail is red with darker rings.

Body   The body is very similar to that of the Turkish Angora, robust and rather elongated, with muscular shoulders, but essentially it is a delicate cat.

Head   Wedge-shaped, with large, hairy ears, pinkish on the inside. The nose is long with a colored tip; the pads are similarly tinted pink.

Eyes   Round, amber-yellow in color.

Tail   Very dense, reddish over the length of it.

Character   Since it became a house cat centuries ago, this breed has remained tranquil, affectionate, intelligent. When born and reared near a lake, it is not afraid of the water and swims well, and so can be easily bathed in lukewarm water, seemingly to its great delight.

Ideal owner   Affectionate toward the entire family, however, the Turkish Van usually has its favorite.

Environment   A house cat, its best surroundings might be an apartment with a terrace with a few plants.

Care   Combing and brushing similar to that required for the Persian.

Reproduction   This is not a very prolific breed; the female produces about four kittens to a litter.

Faults   Excessive markings on body rather than on head and tail, poor musculature, round head.

Top and Bottom: Only color recognized

American Shorthair Silver Tabby Classic Pattern

15 ABYSSINIAN

Origin The mummified remains of some ancient Egyptian cats and reproductions of them in frescoes in tombs were compared with living cats in Abyssinia (which is Ethiopia today) at the end of the nineteenth century. An almost perfect similarity between them was discovered, especially the tawny hair, golden at the roots, and the cranial structure. This explains the widespread belief that today's Abyssinian breed is the direct descendant of the Egyptian cats who were models for the images of the famous goddess Bast.

An English military command brought some of these cats from Abyssinia to England in approximately 1860. The tom was called Zula, and through his merit and with the patience of the breeders Abyssinian cats multiplied easily.

It was only in 1929 that standards for the breed were set. The Abyssinian Club was formed to popularize the breed and continues even today to improve the physical and behavioral characteristics of the cat. "It is not a question of a simple cat," it is said, "but of his majesty, the cat."

During the First and Second World Wars, the lack of proper food caused the almost total extinction of the breed, which in 1960 and 1970 was stricken severely by the feline leukemia virus. Today, the Abyssinian is one of the most sought after and loved cats, particularly in North America.

Coat The hair is short, but the fur is thick like that of rabbits.

Color It can resemble the color of a hare (Ruddy Abyssinian) or it can be copper colored with striations of darker red (Red Abyssinian). There exist also blue or cream varieties, but they are very rare and are not accepted in America.

The curious characteristic of the Abyssinian is that each hair has a light section at the root and a darker section at the tip (ticking), so that the overall effect is a fur of attractive, nuanced shades. The coat of the Abyssinian is sometimes embellished with unwanted delicate bands of cream at the chin, lips, and around the eyes. An undesirable light spotting on the head can give the Abyssinian the appearance of a small, domesticated puma.

Body The body is long and slender, harmonious in its proportions. The slender legs, the small feet with black pads, and its agile movements all combine to give the Abyssinian the elegance of the Siamese.

Head Slightly triangular, delicate, elongated. The nose is dark with a black border. The ears are large and pointed, open, and rounded at the tips.

Eyes They may be green, hazel, or yellow. Their eyes have been described as "the biggest, most innocent eyes in the world."

Tail Long, finely tapered, with thick hair.

Character Very affectionate, sweet, the Abyssinian is nevertheless a lively, athletic, even rambunctious cat. At first contact with a new family, it may seem unsociable, but if treated with respect and addressed in a quiet voice, it quickly shows its good temper and finds expression for its sharp

Top: Ruddy (usual)
Bottom: Red (sorrel)

intelligence. It takes a great interest in everything about the house and meows musically.

Ideal owner   It is necessary that the Abyssinian be given very special attention by an owner who will indulge and play with it. Otherwise the cat will become saddened and tend to isolate itself and even run away. Few cats need as much affectionate attention as Abyssinians, and often they tend to attach themselves to only one person.

Environment   The Abyssinian is not a good apartment cat. It should have at least a terrace or a small garden, while being able to feel the constant presence of the owner. This cat climbs trees like a little panther and expects to be admired for this ancestral talent.

Diet   The Abyssinian is a glutton for meat of every kind. To avoid excessive weight gain (resulting in the loss of its sinuous beauty) do not give it more than 4 to 6 oz. a day, completing the meal with cooked vegetables and a little boiled rice. It also likes ½ tbsp. of brewer's yeast sprinkled on top of the food. During the growing period a vitamin supplement is advisable.

Care   To keep the cat's coat in good condition it should be brushed and rubbed with a cloth every day. The coat will stay soft and shiny in this way.

Reproduction   Males and females living in the same house demonstrate a very touching affection for one another. The females, besides not being very prolific, experience rather difficult pregnancies, for which reason they need assistance at the time of delivery. The female must be watched during her pregnancy because she remains considerably lively; falls must be avoided because fractures occur easily in this highly bred cat. At the most, three to four kittens are born with dark marks on their coat, which disappear after a few months. The development of the kittens is slower than in the majority of other breeds.

Training   With much patience on the part of the owner, the Abyssinian can learn some tricks or simple games. In cat shows, almost conscious of its special charm, it comes to the fore, moving with elegance, playing the part of the beauty, meowing with expressive sweetness.

Faults   Excessive cobbiness; neck marked with white; random spots, rings, and stripes on the legs, neck, and tail.

Ruddy (usual)

Origin   Emigrants who were leaving Europe in the 1600s to seek a new life in America packed up their few belongings, which included their cats, and set sail. These animals make no pretense to nobility, but are simple, domestic creatures. A group of ardent breeders, masterfully adding the blood of some good local stock, succeeded in fixing a new breed: strong, beautiful, original, they were admired and subsequently well received in shows.

The common European cat, which came in with the immigrants, thus obtained its new American nationality with some glory. The first American Shorthair, dated 1904, was named Buster Brown. He was bred from British and American Shorthairs.

Coat   The American Shorthair has short fur of a strong texture, and thus can comfortably stand cold, dampness, battle wounds, and contact with thorny vegetation. During the winter months the fur gets thicker but not woolly.

Color   The Shorthair, so typically American, comes in a full variety of colors.

White: Pure glistening white with eyes of blue or gold or one blue and one gold.

Black: Coal black from the roots to the tips with no rust or smoky color anywhere. The eyes are gold.

Blue: A solid, even blue (gray) from the roots to the tips, nose to tail. A sound lighter shade is preferred to a sound darker shade. The eyes are gold.

Red: A deep, rich, clear, brilliant red with no variations or ticking. This color is particularly difficult to achieve. The eyes are gold.

Cream: One even shade of buff cream, the lighter the better. The eyes are gold.

Chinchilla: The undercoat, chin, ear tufts, stomach, and chest are pure white. The longer hairs on the back, flanks, head, and tail are tipped with black to give a sparkling silver appearance. The rims of the eyes, lips, and nose are outlined with black. The nose itself is brick red; the paw pads are black and the eyes are green or blue-green.

Shaded Silver: This cat is like the Chinchilla in every way except that the black tipping is much heavier, appearing dark on the top and down the back, fading to white on the undersides.

Shell Cameo (Red Chinchilla): This Cameo is red where the Chinchilla is black, including the nose, paw pads, and rims of the eyes. The eyes are gold.

Shaded Cameo (Red Shaded): This Cameo is red where the Shaded Silver is black, including the nose, paw pads, and rims of the eyes. The eyes are gold.

Top: Black
Bottom: Silver Tabby

Black Smoke: This cat appears black when lying still, but when it moves one can see the white undercoat. The eyes are gold.

Blue Smoke: Where the Black Smoke is black this cat is gray with gold eyes.

Cameo Smoke: Where the Black Smoke is black this cat is red with gold eyes.

All the Tabby varieties can be bred in either the Classic Tabby, Mackerel Tabby, or Patched Tabby patterns.

Classic Tabby Pattern

Markings dense, clearly defined, and broad. Legs evenly barred with bracelets rising up to meet the body markings. Tail evenly ringed. Several unbroken necklaces on neck and upper chest, the more the better. Frown marks on forehead form intricate letter "M". Unbroken line runs back from outer corner of eye. Swirls on cheeks. Vertical lines over back of head extend to shoulder markings, which are in the shape of a butterfly with both upper and lower wings distinctly outlined and marked with dots inside outline. Back markings consist of a vertical line down the spine from butterfly to tail with a vertical stripe paralleling it on each side, the three stripes well separated by stripes of the ground color. Large solid blotch on each side to be encircled by one or more unbroken rings. Side markings should be the same on both sides. Double vertical row of buttons on chest and stomach.

Mackerel Tabby Pattern

Markings dense, clearly defined, and all narrow pencillings. Legs evenly barred with narrow bracelets rising up to meet the body markings. Tail barred. Necklaces on neck and chest distinct, like so many chains. Head barred with an "M" on the forehead. Unbroken lines running back from the eyes. Lines running down the head to meet the shoulders. Spine lines run together to form a narrow saddle. Narrow pencillings run around body.

Patched Tabby Pattern

A Patched Tabby (Torbie) is an established silver, brown, or blue tabby with patches of red and/or cream.

Brown Patched Tabby: Coppery brown coat with Classic or Mackerel Tabby black markings and patches of red and/or cream, gold eyes.

Blue Patched Tabby: Bluish-ivory coat with Classic or Mackerel Tabby dark gray markings and patches of cream, gold eyes.

Silver Patched Tabby: Pale silver coat with Classic or Mackerel Tabby black markings and patches of red and/or cream, gold or hazel eyes.

Silver Tabby: Pale silver coat with black markings, black paw pads, red nose, and green or hazel eyes.

Top: White
Bottom: Blue-Cream

Red Tabby: Red coat with dark red markings and red lips, chin, nose, and paw pads, gold eyes.

Brown Tabby: Coppery-brown coat with black markings, red nose, and gold eyes.

Blue Tabby: Bluish-ivory coat with dark gray markings and gold eyes.

Cream Tabby: Light cream coat with darker buff or cream markings, pink nose, paw pads, and gold eyes.

Cameo Tabby: Off-white coat with red markings, rose nose and paw pads and gold eyes.

Tortoiseshell: Black coat with patches of red and cream and gold eyes.

Calico: White coat with patches of black and red, gold eyes.

Dilute Calico: White coat with patches of blue and cream, gold eyes.

Blue-Cream: Gray coat with patches of cream, gold eyes.

Bi-Color: White with patches of black or blue or red or cream, gold eyes.

Body   Solid structure with well-developed chest and shoulders. The sturdy legs and strong feet allow it to navigate even the roughest terrain. It has the aspect of a well-trained athlete, without timidities or fears.

Head   Full with round cheeks, erect ears, substantial whiskers. It is a great hunter, with such powerful jaws that it is able to seize any prey.

Eyes   Brilliant, attentive, lively, rounded but slightly slanting at the outsides.

Character   Intelligent, affectionate, home-loving, likes children. An excellent climber and jumper, it exercises its irrepressible instinct of a hunter even when fully fed. It is ready to catch mice of any size at any time. It is definitely considered a "working cat."

Ideal owner   It attaches itself without exception to every member of the family as long as they treat it with respect and they praise it when it brings home some "little gift" caught on the run.

Environment   It does not scorn apartment life as long as it is occasionally given the liberty to move around on a terrace or a roof. But it would be happy with more ample space. Even if it disappears for some hours, its strong sense of orientation and its love of home make it return punctually to its owners.

Diet   Without problems. If it does not have the opportunity to hunt, it must be given a meal of giblets once a week.

Top: Shaded Silver
Bottom: Red Tabby

Care Requires a good brushing when it comes home. If accustomed to it from a kitten, it does not rebel against a bath with soap and water.

Reproduction Usually produces four kittens in a litter.

Faults Thin or obese body, hair that is too long or too lightweight, an abnormal or very short tail, nose indentation, extra toes, random white spots.

Top: Brown Tabby
Bottom: Red Mackerel Tabby

17 AMERICAN WIREHAIR

Origin The American Wirehair is a modern cat, the fruit of a spontaneous mutation, which happened in 1966 in Verona, New York. Two American Shorthair kittens were born with wiry and curly hair, more similar to that of a lamb than of a kitten. Successive crosses by masterful breeders gave origin to the new breed. For the record: the first American Wirehair was named Adam and he was white and red.

Coat Curly or hooked hair, which forms medium-length fur, coarser on the head, back, flanks, and at the base of the tail, but soft on the chin and underbelly. The look of the coat makes the American Wirehair a very unique cat.

Color Most of the colors of the American Shorthair are permissible except patched tabbies.

Body Of medium size, well proportioned, but stocky and muscular. Strong legs, oval and compact feet. The males are noticeably larger than the females.

Head In proportion to the body, round with prominent cheeks. Gently curving nose and medium ears, rounded.

Eyes Luminous, round, quite wide-set, of a color harmonious with the coat.

Character Independent, profoundly interested in everything around it, affectionate, good mouser, active, agile, capable of dominating other cats with "iron paws."

Ideal owner Attaches itself to the entire family, but likes respect and tranquility.

Environment Home-loving but also fond of open spaces.

Care Brush and comb used in moderation, because its hair must have more of a curly look than a wavy one.

Reproduction These cats are excellent parents.

Faults Long or soft coat, crooked tail, colors that might indicate hybridization, too obvious a break in the nose.

Top: Silver Mackerel Tabby
Bottom: White

18   BOMBAY

Origin   This is a modern breed, created in the United States by means of successful crossings between the Burmese and the American Shorthair. Because it resembles a black leopard of India, it was named for the city of Bombay.

Coat   Shorthair, of a close-lying, satiny texture.

Color   Black to the hair roots and very lustrous. It is lighter at birth.

Body   Supple, elongated, of medium size, rather bulky and supported on agile legs with black paw pads. The males are more noticeably robust with respect to the females than in other breeds.

Head   Round, without flat planes, with a chubby face ending in a short muzzle and a well-defined stop. The ears, of medium size, are gently rounded off at the tips and they perk up immediately at the slightest sound. Black nose.

Eyes   Round, yellow or dark copper.

Tail   Elegant, of medium length.

Character   A good companion, quiet, sensitive, affectionate, reserved, intelligent, soft-voiced. It can live its entire life in the house with no need of going outdoors.

Ideal owner   Friendly to the entire family. It demands in exchange to be left in peace and abhors loud noises.

Environment   It is an animal created for apartment life.

Diet   Moderate appetite, because it burns few calories. It likes mainly meat.

Reproduction   Every litter produces a maximum of four to five kittens, which are voracious eaters. The young are light in color and become completely black after the sixth month.

Faults   Curly hair, spots on the coat, short abnormal tail, green eyes, nose or paw pads other than black.

Top and Bottom: Black (only permitted color)

19 BRITISH SHORTHAIR

Origin Because Harrison Weir, the man who first elevated cat-breeding to an art, loved the prolific British street cat so much he almost single-handedly created the British Shorthair. At the end of the nineteenth century the British Shorthair was the most popular cat in the cat shows held at the Crystal Palace in London. However, in the beginning of the twentieth century, the Persian/Longhair arrived on England's shores. The British Shorthair did not regain favor until the 1930s, then lost ground again as did all breeds during the Second World War. In an effort to restore the breed after the war, Persians/Longhairs were introduced into the breeding program but have been successfully bred out again after years of conscientious control. Because the cats' origins are so natural and ancient it tends to be a strong, healthy, intelligent, and dignified breed with skillful hunting abilities.

Coat For hundreds of years (perhaps thousands) the short, dense coats of the British Shorthairs have protected them through all the worst English weather and underbrush.

Color The British Shorthair officially exists in seventeen separate colors. Some are so popular that they are thought of as individual breeds by those unfamiliar with the cat fancy. For instance, the British take great pride in their Blue and are very competitive with the Chartreux (French Blue). The Tabby is often thought to be an individual breed because of its unique markings.

White: This cat can be seen and shown with blue eyes, orange eyes, or one blue and one orange, but there must never be a green rim around any of the colors. That would be a serious fault. The coat must be a pure white with no traces of yellow.

Black: Like the White, the Black must be a pure black with orange eyes and no green rims.

Blue: The British Blue must have no other color in its coat but the deep, vibrant gray the cat fancy calls blue. The nose and the pads on the feet must also be blue. Only the eyes are in contrast with copper or orange.

Cream: These beige colors are very difficult to achieve with no markings or white anywhere. The Cream also has orange eyes.

Classic Tabby Pattern

Diverse colors according to the variety. But the pattern is characteristic: three dark stripes run down along the spinal column, and on the shoulders is a butterfly shape. On the sides appears a spiral in the form of an oyster, and the chest is crossed by two unbroken narrow lines. Even the muzzle has thin stripes converging toward the nose, while the legs and tail are ringed. All the patterns must contrast with the ground color of the coat. (See American Shorthair Tabby for complete description.)

Mackerel Tabby Pattern

The Mackerel pattern is different from the Classic in that the cat looks more like a tiger. Instead of the blotches and butterfly shapes it has a series of narrow lines running ver-

Top: Brown Tabby
Bottom: British Blue

tically down from the spine. (See American Shorthair Mackerel Tabby for complete description.)

Silver Tabby: Silver coat with black markings. It should have green or hazel eyes, a red or black nose, but no white on it anywhere.

Red Tabby: Dark orange coat with very clear red markings. Round copper eyes.

Brown Tabby: Brown or tawny coat with thick black markings. Orange, hazel, or yellow eyes.

Spotted: A classic tabby with spots all through the design. It can be silver with black spots, brown with black spots, red with deep red spots. It should not have white anywhere.

Tortoiseshell: Black with well-defined patches of cream and red. The nose and pads can be pink or black, the eyes copper or orange. There must be no tabby, white, or unequal balance of color anywhere.

Tortoiseshell and White: Black, cream, and red patches on a white coat. The eyes should be copper or orange. There should be some white on the paws but there should always be more tri-colored patches than white.

Blue-Cream: A mix of blue and cream patches. There should be an even mixture of the colors, especially on the paws. The eyes must be copper or orange with no green rims.

Bi-Color: Any solid color and white together. Copper or orange eyes with no green rims.

Smoke: A black or blue cat with a pale silver undercoat. There must be no tabby or white in the coat. The eyes are yellow or orange.

British Tipped: This cat has a white undercoat with the coat on the back, flanks, head, ears, and tail tipped with any of the recognized solid colors, including chocolate and lilac. The chin, chest, and stomach remain white. The eye colors change according to the color of the tipping. There may be some vestigial tail rings, but no other Tabby markings should be present.

Body This is a massive, well-built, well-proportioned cat with a broad chest and a compact body on short, strong legs.

Head A massive, round head should sit on a short, thick neck. The nose must always be straight and broad. The ears and the eyes are set wide apart, and the chin is firm and strong.

Eyes Big, round, open, and even.

Tail Short, thick, and rounded at the tip. In good proportion to the body.

Character This strong cat has a sense of responsibility, dignity, independence, and yet loves its family dearly. It will play with children and dogs and be a loyal companion to adults. Because of its inner strength it can handle all situations with great aplomb.

Ideal owner The British Shorthair loves all who love it.

Environment Although it may prefer a large space with gardens and terrain, it can adapt to almost any reasonable surroundings.

Faults Irregular tail, nose stop, or a long or fluffy coat.

Top: Orange-Eyed White
Bottom: Brown Spotted Tabby

Origin There is a legend that this breed comes from Burman monasteries where it was venerated as a divinity. A book of poems from the Ayudhya period (1350–1767) of Siam (Thailand) describes a Burmese cat, a Siamese, a Korat, and a black feline with a white collar named Singhasep.

A female Burmese with a brown coat named Wong Mau was imported from the capital of Rangoon into the United States. Crossed with a male Siamese, a new dynasty originated at the end of the 1920s.

Coat Silky haired, fine, thick, shiny.

Color The Burmese has a brown coat, which in a mature cat becomes dark sable brown. In North America the Burmese is by definition a brown cat, however, Great Britain recognizes the following: Red, Cream, Blue, Lilac, Chocolate, Brown Tortie, Blue Tortie, Chocolate Tortie, and Lilac Tortie.

Body Of medium size, long, graceful, elegant, but muscular and of unexpected strength. It must be totally devoid of fat. Long neck, round chest, slender legs, well-shaped oval feet. Although related to the Siamese, it must not resemble that breed too much.

Head Triangular, short, and narrowing down, and always shorter than that of the Siamese. Pronounced chin, strong jaw. Ears are wide at the base, ending in rounded tips.

Eyes Slanted, inclining toward the nose but wide-set, of a golden yellow color and very expressive.

Tail Long, straight, tapering at the tip.

Character Affectionate, intelligent, desirous of attention and praise, lovable, very inquisitive. It loves to travel in a car or on a train and delights in looking out of the windows without becoming frightened. It has a rather loud voice.

Ideal owner It is necessary that the Burmese have an owner who knows how to return the cat's affection and who will dedicate some time to play with it and pet it. It is sociable with familiar persons and with strangers.

Environment It has a great capacity to adapt itself, for which reason the Burmese is both a city and a country cat. It lives well in an apartment, especially if there is a terrace with green plants.

Diet It is a healthy and strong cat, and does not require special attention. Meals of meat, vegetables, a little rice, and vitamins during the growing period.

Care The coat must always be kept clean, gently stroking it with a flannel or a glove dampened with water or vinegar.

Reproduction The female goes into her first heat at the age of seven months and the average litter numbers five. The kittens are born with coffee-colored coats, which then darken. The Burmese is a long-lived cat and can live to eighteen years old.

Top: Sable Brown (only color recognized in USA)
Bottom: Chocolate Brown (British Standard)

Faults White marks under the throat, patterns or lines on the coat, colors that are too dark, gray or green eyes, curved or kinky tail.

Varieties In North America the Blue, Champagne (Chocolate), and Platinum (Lilac) Burmese are called Malayans and belong to a separate breed. (Please see the Malayan section.)

Left and right: Sable Brown

Origin Mysterious, but certainly French. According to the most believable hypothesis, a cat bred in the monasteries of the Carthusian monks, probably in one of their monasteries near Paris. However, it must be considered a fairly old breed, because botanist Carolus Linnaeus (1707–1778) already spoke of Chartreux/British Blue cats in his writings. During the same period the name of the breed is mentioned in the Universal Dictionary of Animals by the naturalist Georges Louis Leclerc de Buffon.

Coat Short-haired, dense, velvety, glossy, similar to that of the otter.

Color All shades of gray are permitted, the lightest gray being the most highly prized. The skin is completely blue. The French writer Colette wrote of her Chartreux: "The sun played on her Chartreux coat, mauve and blue like a woodpigeon's neck."

Body Powerful and massive, it can weigh up to 13 or 14 lbs. Wide shoulders and chest, a stocky neck, muscular legs. But it has a noble gait, similar to that of wild felines. Compared with the female, the male gives the impression of great strength.

Head Rounded skull, triangular muzzle, straight nosed, highset ears, full cheeks, pronounced jaws, almost black lips.

Eyes Round, golden or copper, amber-yellow or orange. They express sweetness, trust, and good naturedness.

Tail Long, sturdy, carried over the back.

Character It is a gentle cat, affectionate, shrewd, independent. All good qualities of cats and even of dogs are attributed to this cat. It mews little. It is a good mouser.

Ideal owner Its sweetness, likeability, and willingness win over the entire family. It becomes fond of everyone who treats it with respect and love.

Environment The optimum would be a large apartment, hopefully with a terrace, attic, and cellar, where it could put into play its great mousing abilities.

Diet Meat with a little rice and vegetables. Giblets once a week. It is advisable to frequently give the cat meat that is cut into cubes; chewing develops the typical Chartreux/British Blue cheeks.

Care Regular brushings. It is a very healthy cat.

Reproduction Unfortunately, the Chartreux/British Blue breed has become rare. But this beautiful, good, and powerful cat has sparked new enthusiasm among breeders.

Faults White hairs, streaks, spots, green eyes, light musculature and skeleton

Varieties Three types are found in France: purebred with no foreign blood; those which have Persian Blue in their ancestry; those which have British Blue forebears, the English version of the Chartreux.

Distant cats have been reported to be similar to the Chartreux/British Blue. The Chorazan province of Persia was supposed to have had a deep gray and not very sociable cat. And Tobolsk, Russia (in Siberia) may have had a long, woolly, dark red-haired cat.

Top: Kitten
Bottom: Blue

Origin The original Siamese had a fawn-color coat with seal brown points. Points are the face mask, ears, legs, feet, and tail. It was later bred with Chocolate, Lilac, and Blue points, which were accepted in the breed in the United States. But when the Siamese was crossed with Abyssinians and other Shorthairs to achieve a wider array of point colors, the American organizations felt that they should be classed in a separate breed because of the genes coming from the non-Siamese. The British continued to class the new colors as Siamese. Thus was born the Colorpoint Shorthair.

Coat Short, close-lying, fine, and glossy.

Color The Colorpoint Shorthair includes the following:

Red Point: White coat with dark red points.

Cream Point: White coat with apricot points.

Seal-Lynx Point: Fawn coat with tabby points in light and dark brown.

Chocolate-Lynx Point: Ivory coat with tabby points in very light and medium brown.

Blue-Lynx Point: Bluish white coat with tabby points in contrasting shades of gray.

Lilac-Lynx Point: White coat with tabby points in contrasting shades of pinkish gray.

Red-Lynx Point: White coat with tabby points in contrasting shades of red.

Seal-Tortie Point: Fawn coat with brown points mottled with red and cream.

Chocolate-Cream Point: Ivory coat with brown points mottled with cream.

Blue-Cream Point: Bluish white coat with dark gray points mottled with cream.

Lilac-Cream Point: White coat with pinkish gray points mottled with cream.

All the other characteristics of the Colorpoint Shorthair are the same as the Siamese.

Chocolate Lynx Point

Origin   This cat is unique because its history probably goes back to ancient Egypt as it is pictured as early as 1400 B.C. It is also uniquely spotted like no other natural breed of domestic cat. The modern Egyptian Mau dates to 1953 when Princess Natalie Troubetskoye imported a female Egyptian to Italy where she mated her to another Egyptian and obtained two kittens. The male kitten was later bred back to the mother and the breed began. Princess Troubetskoye brought these cats to America in 1956 and established the breed.

It is called Egyptian Mau because in the ancient Egyptian language "mau" means cat. It is clearly a first cousin of the Abyssinian.

Coat   A fine, textured fur, which is silky, dense, and shiny, formed of medium-length hair.

Color   The dominant feature is the marking pattern. Unlike the Tabby the Egyptian markings are separate, random spots on the body. The markings on the face and head are more like mascara lines, and the tail is banded. The Egyptian comes in three colors:

Silver: Silver coat with charcoal markings and green eyes.

Bronze: Light bronze coat with dark brown markings and green eyes.

Smoke: Gray and silver coat with black markings and green eyes.

Body   Of medium size, proportioned and balanced, elegant, with well-developed musculature. Very long legs.

Head   Slightly rounded and a mildly pointed muzzle. Large ears, which twitch frequently, wide at the base and moderately pointed, with pink insides that give the impression of transparency.

Eyes   Wide, almond-shaped, preferably green but can be yellow or hazel.

Tail   Long and tapering.

Character   Intelligent, wise, docile, a good hunter. Has a melodious, almost birdlike voice.

Ideal owner   It adapts itself very well to almost any sort of domestic life, but it makes friends only with the people it likes.

Environment   It does not require open space, and so can live tranquilly even in a small apartment, better yet if it has a terrace.

Diet   Meat and occasional giblets, with a little rice and vegetables.

Care   It is a rather delicate cat, which is affected by sudden changes in temperature. It requires particular attention during the changes of season.

Reproduction   Whether male or female, they make excellent parents, taking very good care of their young and playing with them for long periods of time. The development of the kittens is rather slow.

Faults   Blended spots or lack of spots, small head, pointed muzzle, eyes that slant too much, short tail, wrong eye color.

Top: Bronze
Bottom: Smoke

Origin The term "European" generically groups all short-haired cats of good quality existing in Europe, provided they are house cats. Millions of families own them.

Their origin is uncertain. It probably descends from the African Wildcat, introduced by the Romans about 2,000 years ago. The European breed dates from remote antiquity and probably constitutes the purest of the feline breeds because it has retained the ancestral characteristics without the need of breeders and genetic studies.

The name "Tabby" comes from Iraq. Jewish weavers of Baghdad copied the colors and designs of the coats of these cats in the silks they sent to Europe. These precious fabrics were sold under the name tabby. The cat is also known as Marbled Cat, Cyprus Cat, and Tiger Cat.

The individual colors of the European Shorthair are considered separate breeds, acknowledging the different genes required to achieve the different colors.

Coat Short, fine, compact hair, which is sometimes bristly.

Color The standards permit many colors and patterns.

European Black: A beautiful and widespread breed. It has a glossy black coat and splendid yellow, orange, or copper eyes. It is a courageous and combative animal. Defects of the breed include: triangular head, brownish color, spots, and white hairs. The kittens show traces of streakings at birth, which disappear later. Black cats with green eyes are not acceptable.

European White: A most beautiful animal but less widespread than the Black. There exist types with yellow, orange, or copper eyes. The blue-eyed type, quite rare, is almost always deaf; the type with one eye a different color from the other is considered the best sire because it can father either blue-eyed kittens or those with orange or copper eyes. Faulty European Whites are those with eyes of an indefinable color, pointed muzzle, yellowish coat, or fragile legs. It is authoritative and combative. Care of the coat requires brushings with talcum powder.

European Albino: There also exists a type of European White with light blue eyes and pupils with red reflections. The advantage of this albino cat is that it does not become deaf. Although registered as a breed, the albinos are not allowed in shows.

European Cream: It is also very rare. Streaked or reddish coat indicates mediocrity. The ideal type must have a spotless cream coat, round head, and hazel or copper eyes.

European Red: Bright red, with uniform, orange eyes. Rare breed.

European Gray: Well bred in England and very widespread. It is of a solid build, light gray, uniform coat, and copper or orange eyes.

European Tabby: Resembles a tiger in miniature and is highly prized. It has a stocky body, massive and muscular. Strong head and pronounced cheeks. Broad shoulders. The stripes in the coat can be in continuous lines or lines broken with a tawny or brown color. It is a real companion, and very

Top: Red Spotted
Bottom: Blue

useful for its ruthless mania for mousing. This pattern closely resembles the Mackerel Tabby in America.

European Marbled: It has a more elongated body than the Tabby, and cheeks that are not too pronounced. From the nape of the neck to the tail, the back is crossed by three black bands. On the shoulders there are two black blotches in the shape of butterflies. On the flanks there are two fan-shaped whorls. There is an infinite variety of colors permitted. It is a cat which knows how to hunt mice of every size, snakes, green lizards, birds, little mammals, even fish. This pattern closely resembles the Classic Tabby in America.

European Tortoiseshell: A variety that is almost exclusively female. Its coat has a turtle shell design and is comprised of well-distinguished and bright black, red, and cream. Orange, copper, or hazel eyes. It has a reputation for bringing good luck. If a male is born, an exceptional fact, he is sterile. Therefore, reproduction is accomplished through a European stud of a solid color that corresponds to one of the three colors of the turtle shell.

European Tortoiseshell with White: Black, red, cream in large, well-defined spots, with white areas on the muzzle and chest. Orange, copper, or amber eyes. The females are particularly affectionate.

European Blue-Cream: A result of crossings between European Cream and European Blue. Therefore, the coat of this breed should appear as a mixture of blue and cream, without either color dominating. Orange, yellow, or copper eyes. It is an exclusively female variety.

European Bi-Color: Black and white, white and blue, orange and white, cream and white, with colored ears and mask. The whole of the coat must not appear more than two-thirds white.

Body Well constructed, massive, solid, muscular, with a broad chest, sturdy legs, round feet, well planted on the ground.

Head Round with developed cheeks, little ears rounded at the tips, short nose.

Eyes Large, expressive, the color varying with the coat.

Character It is an active, intelligent, shrewd, lively, courageous, inquisitive cat. A good mouser and hunter of other small animals. Since many of these cats are born outside of breeding controls, the character of the European Shorthair can vary greatly, although it always shows a definite domesticity as opposed to its wild progenitors. It resists the cold and lives long. It has a gentle voice.

Ideal owner The European Shorthair is a cat which adapts itself to any kind of life, as long as its owners love it and respect its habits. In particular the female attaches itself closely to the whole family. It is, however, an animal which likes activity and company.

Environment Apartment, terrace, garden, and large spaces are all suitable to the life of the European Shorthair.

Diet Without problems. It eats everything, with preferences for milk and meat.

Top: White
Bottom left:
    Silver Marbled
Bottom right:
    Spotted Silver

Reproduction If the females are not carefully watched when they are in heat, these popular felines can reproduce more frequently and with larger litters than other breeds. The kittens begin to eat meat very early.

Origin It was bred in the 1960s by crossing a Persian/Longhair with an American Shorthair.

Coat It is longer than that of other short-haired cats. The fur is dense, soft, almost silky. However, it does not lie too close to the body, but is springy, almost alive.

Color They are the same colors that are permitted for the Persian/Longhair with a few exceptions: Golden, the Persian Van Bi-Color, and the Peke-Face Red. (See the Persian/Longhair section for complete descriptions.)

Body Sturdy and elegant, with strong and muscular legs.

Head Massive, with a chubby face and a muscular neck. The little ears are set in the roundness of the face. The nose is short and broad, with a stop. Overall, it looks like a Persian Shorthair.

Eyes Round, bright, expressive, a bit wide-set, giving its face a sweet expression. They must be blue in the white-haired variety and copper in the black-haired variety, however, always conforming to the coat color.

Tail Short, low set, without curves.

Character It is a very intelligent cat, sweet, gentle, affectionate, pensive, and a good mouser.

Ideal owner It is the whole family's cat.

Environment It is the classic apartment cat, a place to which it remains tied with deep affection.

Diet Meat, giblets, and vegetables in limited quantities to avoid weight gain.

Care Easy brushing.

Reproduction Litters of four are the usual, and the young are born with darker coats than the parents, reaching their full beauty only at maturity.

Faults Delicate head, short or abnormal tail, and eyes which do not match the color of the coat.

Top: Red Tabby
Bottom: Tortoiseshell

Origin We owe the birth of this breed to the fortuitous mating of a black shorthair female and a male Chocolate Point Siamese in 1952. The cat born of that union was in turn crossed with another Chocolate Point Siamese. But in the simple formula, held secret, it seems that Russian Blue was introduced.

The name Havana Brown was given the new breed by the English not because the breeding took place in Cuba (it took place in England), but because the cat's color was similar to that of the tobacco used in the famous Havana cigar. It is an acceptable hypothesis. But at the end of the 1950s, in order to avoid protests that it might not be of British origin and confusion with the Havana rabbit used in fur manufacturing, the Havana Brown was baptized Chestnut Brown. But in the last few years the original name of this breed has again been used.

The Havana Brown in America is not nearly so Siamese in type. The British Havana looks much more like the American Chestnut Oriental Shorthair.

Coat Medium, glossy, smooth, uniform over the body.

Color To do honor to the British name of Chestnut, all shades of chestnut brown are permitted. The color must be uniform all over the body. Even the nose and the whiskers have the same color as the coat. The only exception is the pink of the paw pads.

Body Medium length, elegant, muscular. This cat should not be too stocky or too svelte. The legs are medium length.

Head Long muzzle, longer than it is wide, tapering gradually to a strong chin. Wide-set, forward-tilted, round-tipped ears.

Eyes Oval-shaped, green, shining.

Tail Medium long, tapering.

Character Lively, very playful, lordly, reservedly affectionate, ideal companion, home-loving. It has a courteous voice, but the mother tends to speak constantly with her kittens. Becoming acquainted with this cat will illustrate that it is different from other breeds.

Ideal owner This is a one-person pet for someone who wants a faithful companion without excessive manifestations.

Environment Apartment, preferably with a small terrace.

Diet Normal. It is a healthy cat.

Care It is necessary to brush the coat and shine it with a flannel or a glove in the direction of the hair growth. No other special attention is required.

Reproduction The female is an excellent mother. The kittens are born with fine fur like that of a child's plush toy, and their eyes open within the first week. It is still a rare breed, for which reason the price is high.

Faults Tiger markings, spots, white hairs on the coat, short or hooked tail, sturdy and round head.

Top and bottom: Chestnut Brown

Origin   It is a cat known for centuries in Japan. At first there appeared the black, then the white, and finally the red. When the Bobtail was born with all three of these colors, it became the symbol of good luck and was named *Mi-Ke* (pronounced *Me-Ka*, meaning three colors). It often appears in oriental literature and paintings. Good-luck charms show it with a raised paw, a courteous and kind gesture. The breed spread to other continents after the Second World War, and was brought to the United States by the American Armed Forces. However, the breed is rare.

Coat   It has a medium-length fur, soft as silk but strong, with little undercoat.

Color   Black, white, and red are preferred whether as a single color or in double or triple combinations, as long as the division of color is sharp and the white predominates. However, the only colors not allowed are the Siamese and Abyssinian patterns.

Body   Lean, elegant, but well-muscled frame.

Head   In the form of an almost equilateral triangle, with a slightly rounded muzzle and broad, upstanding ears.

Eyes   Very bright, oval-shaped, and definitely slanty. They must harmonize with the color of the coat.

Tail   It is one of the cat's distinguishing characteristics. The name "Bobtail" derives from the fact that this Japanese cat possesses a short tail (4 to 5 in. or 10 to 12.5 cm.) Because of its curved position it is barely visible, as with rabbits. It is, however, not related to the cat of the Island of Man, also a tailless cat.

Character   It is a unique cat, affectionate, intelligent, lively, a mouser, inquisitive.

Ideal owner   It becomes attached to the entire family and demands to be respected.

Environment   It is readily adaptable to life both indoors and out.

Diet   It likes fish above everything else, so it is necessary to give it fish at least once a week.

Care   Light daily brushings.

Faults   A round and short head, skeleton and musculature which are too heavy, excessively long tail or one which is not curved.

Top: Mi-ke
Bottom: Black and White

Origin It is one of the first cats mentioned in history. (See the Burmese section.) It originated in the province of Korat in Thailand, and was known by the name of *Si-Sawat* and considered to be good luck. At one time it was customary to give one to princes and notables as a sign of devotion.

A male and female were imported to the United States in 1959. The breed was officially recognized in 1966, and it reached Europe only in 1972. Today's Korat is identical to the ancient one as seen throughout the centuries in old representations.

Coat Thick, soft, silky, glossy, close-fitting with no undercoat.

Color Solid silver-blue without variants or streaks. *Si-Sawat* in the language of Thailand means a light green-gray or silver.

Head Heart-shaped, with a tapering but not pointed muzzle. Wide ears with rounded tips, erect and always alert.

Eyes Large, prominent, luminous, enigmatic, of a beautiful green or amber-green. This is a fundamental characteristic of the breed.

Tail Of medium length, strong at the root and blunted at the tip.

Character Affectionate, intelligent, combative, profoundly aware of everything around it. The females, in particular, maintain their playfulness until old age.

Ideal owner It lives better with calm people. It has a sweet and soft voice. It is intolerant of strange cats in the house.

Environment Strictly an apartment cat, it does not like street noises or a hectic household.

Diet Chiefly meat.

Care A daily massage of the coat with a flannel glove. It is necessary to vaccinate this cat against viral infections of the respiratory system.

Reproduction Both female and male are very attached to their young, and they care for the kittens together with love. The kittens reach their full beauty only after they have reached the age of two years old.

Training The Korat is easily tamable and is willing to learn tricks, seeming very happy to perform them.

Faults Colors which are not definitely silver-blue, and a tail that is curly at the tip.

Top: Silver-Blue—kitten
Bottom: Silver-Blue

Origin A recent, strictly American breed, officially recognized in 1980. It is a twin of the Burmese, from which it differs only in color. In Great Britain the Malayan colors are considered Burmese.

Coat Fine, glossy, short, satiny.

Color This is a mostly even, solid-colored cat. The colors are: champagne—a warm beige; blue—a medium gray with fawn undertones; platinum—a light silver with fawn undertones.

Body Of medium size, muscular, compact, devoid of fat. Round, broad chest and slender legs.

Head Pleasantly rounded and without flat areas, a very visible stop in profile, a full face.

Eyes Yellow, round, wide-set.

Tail Straight, of medium length.

Character Very affectionate, lovable, inquisitive, strong willed. It loves to travel and has a loud voice.

Ideal owner It needs an owner who can return its affection, dedicates a great deal of time to it, and holds and fondles it frequently. It is sociable with familiars and with strangers.

Environment It is comfortable in a spacious apartment with a planted terrace if possible. It hates loud noises.

Diet Meals of meat, vegetables, rice, and vitamins during the growing period. It is a healthy cat.

Care Keep the coat always clean and shiny by stroking it with a flannel or a glove.

Reproduction The females go into their first heat at about seven to eight months old. Although it is registered as a separate breed, the Malayan can be born spontaneously of Burmese parents. One kittening can produce both Burmese and Malayan young. The Malayan is a long-lived cat.

Faults Blue or green eyes; white spots or streaks; a truncated, crooked, or kinky tail.

Champagne

Origin There is a story that Phoenicians, capable merchants and Mediterranean navigators, spread these cats from Japan, China, and Malaysia where the breed was perfected. Ancient paintings include some examples of tailless cats, the singular characteristic of today's Manx. However, breeders currently believe that the Japanese Bobtail carries a recessive bobtail gene that breeds bobtails every time, while the Manx tailless gene is dominant and will cause stillbirths if not bred to a tailed cat.

In 1588, a galleon of the invincible Spanish Armada, which carried some tailless cats on board (there are always some mice on ships), sank off the Irish coast, near the Isle of Man. Segregated on this island, the breed developed by itself, and breeders made sure that cats of diverse origin did not mate with these tailless felines. The characteristic became hereditary within several generations, and many kittens began to be born without tails. Legend has it that this cat was late getting to Noah's Ark, arriving just at the instant in which the great patriarch was closing the main entrance, and so its tail was cut off and carried away by the waters of the flood. A more recent legend tells that Irish warriors used to embellish their battle helmets with tails cut from felines of the Isle of Man. Thus, a mother cat delicately bit off the little tails of her newborns to alleviate the pain of the future mutilation of her kittens.

A club was founded in 1901. Since that time, even though the reproduction of the Manx is limited, fanciers from every part of the world can obtain one. The inhabitants of the island are so proud of their national feline that they have minted a coin with its image.

Coat Its fur is double, shiny, clean, with light, soft hair like that of a rabbit. It has a dense undercoat.

Color As in the case of the European Shorthair, all colors are permitted. Therefore, there are solid-color, bi-color, tabby, marbled, and tortoiseshell Manx cats.

Body Muscular, with a rounded rump, deep, full flanks, and short back. The hind legs are longer than the forelegs, so that its walk resembles a rabbit's hop.

Head Imposing, wide, round, with well-developed cheeks, short, strong neck, long nose, and wide-set ears, which are slightly rounded.

Eyes Wide, round, bright. Any color is permissible as long as it matches the color of the coat.

Tail The Manx with its cousin the Cymric are the only tailless breeds of cat. At the point where the tail should begin, one finds a small, natural subsidence (hollow), sometimes covered with a tuft of hair. Although this lack of tail is a unique characteristic, it also slightly diminishes its beauty. Moreover, it is a handicap because it compromises the balance of the animal.

Top: Brown Classic Tabby
Bottom: Brown Mackerel Tabby—kitten

Character   It is an intelligent cat, docile, happy, very playful, and active. Endowed with excellent reflexes, it is a ruthless mouser.

Ideal owner   The Manx never has a single owner because it is friendly with the family and whomever frequents the house. It is comfortable with everyone.

Environment   It is a decidedly home-loving animal. The house is its sole kingdom and it rarely makes sorties for reasons of wanderlust. However, when it does go out, it exhibits an excellent ability to climb trees.

Diet   Normal cat food, without special preferences. Weight gain should be avoided.

Care   It should be brushed frequently, but very carefully and lightly so as not to ruin the soft, silky hair.

Reproduction   Breeding presents serious problems, both for a certain amount of difficulty in preserving the tailless characteristic and because a continuous cross of two tailless Manx cats could result in malformations of the vertebrae, causing some kittens to die before birth or shortly after. In order that the breed develop strongly, it is necessary to cross some tailless Manx cats with those who have an embryonic tail, or else with a cat who has a normal tail.

Manx kittens at birth show some variabilities divided into four groups: those born completely without a tail; those with a small protuberance; those with a little tail (which can be amputated); and those endowed with a tail, even though it is always somewhat smaller than normal. The kittens with these variations are considered pure Manx, but only those without tails can be shown. A Manx gives birth to four young at the most.

Faults   Fur devoid of undercoat, small head.

Varieties   The Cymric (see Cymric section) is a breed created in the 1960s. This is a long-haired cat with a unique appearance—tufts of hair on its ears and cheeks, a soft coat of medium length with an undercoat.

Top: Red Classic Tabby
Bottom: Red Classic Tabby

Origin Like the Egyptian Mau, this cat is spotted rather than having the traditional tabby markings. This *simulated* ocelot was bred from an Abyssinian pointed Siamese and a Chocolate Point Siamese. Although many generations have been bred, it is not yet recognized in the cat fancy. The Ocicat has Abyssinian and Siamese ancestors, but there are also American Shorthairs in its pedigree, so it tends to be a large cat weighing from 12 to 15 lbs.

Coat Short and shiny.

Color A cream coat with either dark or light brown spots and markings.

Body A large, well-muscled cat with long legs.

Head Well-proportioned head with straight lines, a fine muzzle, and large pricked ears.

Eyes Yellow.

Tail Long and tapering.

Character They are very friendly, attention-getting animals reflecting both their Siamese and Abyssinian backgrounds.

Ideal owner It requires people who enjoy having active, beautiful animals.

Environment Large apartments with gardens and terraces are best.

Diet Meat or fish with vegetables and rice.

Care Simple brushing.

Reproduction No remarkable problems though it is a relatively new breed.

Faults Spots blending into tabby pattern.

Top: Bronze
Bottom: Silver

Origin   The Oriental Shorthair is a solid-colored Siamese. It began in America in the mid-1970s, but in England it began in the 1960s as the Foreign Shorthair. In truth, it began with the Siamese cat centuries ago. The Colorpoint cats that we know as Siamese are merely a portion of the Siamese breed as it is known in Thailand (Siam). In that country there are cats of many different solid colors, all with the same Siamese physical shape known as "foreign." When these solid-colored Siamese were excluded from the Siamese breed in England in the 1920s, their breeders created new breeds for them called "Foreign." Each color is referred to as an individual breed in England and Europe, so they are known as Foreign White, Foreign Lilac, etc. The breed has reached new heights in America with twenty-six separate colors.

Coat   Short, fine, close-lying, and glossy.

Color   Unlike most other breeds, the Oriental Shorthair colors are grouped into classes: Solid, Shaded, Smoke, Tabby, and Parti-Color.

Solid Colors Class

White: White coat with blue or green eyes preferred. Yellow eyes are allowed but odd-eyed cats are not.

Ebony: Coal black with no other color. Green eyes are preferred but yellow are allowed.

Blue: Gray coat, the lighter the better, but even-colored over the entire body.

Chestnut: Medium-brown coat, even the whiskers and the nose are the same color.

Lavender: An even-colored pinkish gray coat with nose and paw pads of the same color.

Red: Bright red over the entire cat.

Cream: Buff-cream coat, the lighter the better, with pink nose and paw pads.

Shaded Colors Class

Silver: White undercoat with longer hairs tipped with ebony, blue, chestnut, or lavender. The rims of the eyes, lips, and nose are lined in black.

Cameo: White undercoat with longer hairs tipped with red.

Smoke Colors Class

Ebony Smoke: White undercoat heavily tipped with black. When the cat is lying still, it appears to be black.

Blue Smoke: White undercoat heavily tipped with gray. When the cat is lying still, it appears to be all gray.

Chestnut Smoke: White undercoat heavily tipped with brown. When the cat is lying still, it appears to be brown.

Lavender Smoke: White undercoat heavily tipped with pinkish gray. When the cat is lying still, it appears to be lavender.

Cameo Smoke: White undercoat heavily tipped with red. When the cat is lying still, it appears to be red.

Tabby Colors Class

In addition to the Classic and Mackerel Tabby patterns (see American Shorthair for full descriptions), the Oriental

Top: Lavender
Bottom: Cream

Shorthair is also bred in the Spotted and Ticked Tabby patterns. The pattern can be seen in any of the Tabby colors.

Spotted Tabby Pattern

Markings on the body should be spotted. They may vary in size and shape with preference given to round, evenly distributed spots. Spots should not run together in a broken Mackerel pattern. A dorsal stripe is ideally composed of spots. The markings of the face and forehead should be typically Tabby markings, with underside of the body having "vest buttons." Legs and tail are barred.

Ticked Tabby Pattern

The body hairs should be ticked with various shades of marking color and ground color; when viewed from the top it should be free from noticeable spots, stripes, or blotches, except for darker dorsal shading. Lighter underside may show tabby markings. Face, legs, and tail must show distinct tabby striping. The cat must have at least one distinct necklace.

Ebony Tabby: Coppery-brown coat with black markings.

Blue Tabby: Bluish white coat with dark gray markings.

Chestnut Tabby: Fawn coat with brown markings.

Lavender Tabby: Pale gray coat with rich, pinkish gray markings.

Red Tabby: Red coat with dark red markings.

Cream Tabby: Pale cream coat with darker buff-cream markings.

Silver Tabby: Light silver coat with black markings.

Cameo Tabby: White coat with red markings.

Parti-Color Colors Class

Tortoiseshell: Black coat with patches of red and cream.

Blue-Cream: Gray coat with patches of cream.

Chestnut-Tortie: Medium-brown coat with patches of red and cream.

Lavender-Cream: Gray coat with patches of cream.

All other characteristics are the same as the Siamese.

Top: Blue
Bottom: Ebony

Origin   The Rex has appeared as a spontaneous mutation several times in various locations in the world: Germany, Ohio, Oregon, and, most particularly, England. When a curly coated cat was born in an otherwise normal litter in Cornwall, England, in 1950, it was taken seriously and bred back to its mother to produce more curly coated kittens. Ten years later another curly coated kitten was found in Devon, England, and bred to the Cornish line, but they could not produce curly coated kittens together. So began the Devon Rex, essentially a different breed from the Cornish since they cannot reproduce their distinctive qualities together. They do, however, share the title of Rex in the cat fancy.

Coat   The Cornish Rex has a curly or wavy undercoat that is very fine, silky, and close fitting with no top coat or longer guard hairs. The Devon Rex also has the fine, silky, curly undercoat, but in addition has a few guard hairs. Even the whiskers are curly on these cats.

Color   Most of the American colors are accepted for competition. Many Siamese colorpointed and solid colors are bred unofficially and called Si-Rex.

Body   Both types have essentially foreign (Siamese) bodies that are medium length, lean, light, but solidly muscular, with an arched back and long, straight legs.

Head   The Cornish has a medium-length triangular head, long straight nose and large ears blending into the triangular shape of the head. The Devon also has a triangular head but fuller cheeks, a shorter nose with a stop (a dip or break in the line), and extremely large, wide-set ears.

Eyes   Oval-shaped, clear, and intense, matching the color of the coat.

Tail   Long, slender at the tip, covered with curly hair.

Character   The Rex is good, responsive, open, tranquil, but capable of agile jumps, inquisitive, affectionate, manageable but independent, and very intelligent. It could be called a lap cat, but it can run very fast.

Ideal owner   It was nicknamed by the English as "an animal suited to gentle owners." Normally it becomes attached to the entire family.

Environment   It is decidedly home-loving, a creature of habit, and therefore most suitable to apartment life.

Diet   It likes meat above all. It is a basically healthy cat, but be careful to avoid excessive weight gain.

Care   Simple repeated strokes of a flannel mitt on the coat.

Reproduction   Only pairs of the same breed and variety must be coupled. If a Cornish Rex is mated with a Devon Rex, kittens with straight hair result. Kittenings produce between three to six young. The kittens become active very soon. When they begin to go out of their little house, they immediately demonstrate an extreme inquisitiveness typical of the breed. The females are ideal mothers.

Faults   Chocolate hybridization or resemblance to oriental colors, kinked tail.

Top: Torby (Tortoiseshell/Tabby)
Bottom: Dilute Calico (Blue-Cream and White)

Origin   The breed was probably imported into England more than a century ago aboard a merchant ship coming from the Russian port of Archangel. The cat was gray, lovable, elegant; with intelligent breeding the English perfected the body lines and made the breed popular. In addition to Russian Blue, it is called Spanish Blue, Archangel, and Maltese. This could mean that the breed spread quickly and was welcomed in various countries.

Coat   Short hair, thick, perfectly uniform, as if it were covered with plush. The undercoat protects the cat from the cold and gives the coat the silvery luster of mink. This is the distinctive character of the breed.

Color   All shades of gray up to blue-gray, evenly distributed. Blue-gray is the color that gives the breed its name.

Body   Rangy, slender, delicately boned, long and slim legs, well-rounded feet. It is not the color but the silhouette that resembles the Egyptian cat of the pharaohs.

Head   A wide face with a medium-long, straight nose and a strong chin. The elongated and sinuous neck gives the cat a touch of special elegance. The ears are broad, pointed, erect, and seem transparent because they have so little hair.

Eyes   Almond-shaped, wide-set eyes must always be green: from light emerald to dark bottle green.

Tail   Long, straight, smooth, and tapering.

Character   It is a very serene, tranquil cat, sweet, demonstratively affectionate, intelligent, and courageous. It mews delicately during mating periods. The Russian Blues are very affectionate with each other and therefore make excellent parents.

Ideal owner   This cat is happy with a serene family, preferably where there are neither restless children nor too much noise.

Environment   It is a typical apartment cat. It spends many winter hours near the stove or the radiator, but if necessary it can stand the cold as did its Russian ancestors.

Diet   It must be varied if possible, composed of chopped meat, lung, vegetables, and some occasional giblets.

Care   The hair must remain upright, and should be brushed that way to avoid flattening the coat.

Reproduction   To obtain an excellent Russian Blue, the parents must be perfectly pure because the breed has a tendency to deteriorate. Every kittening usually produces four young. Strict breeding occurs in the United States and in northern Europe.

Faults   Obesity, wide head, white hairs in the coat, spots, patterns.

Top and bottom: Shades of Russian Blue

Origin The chronicles speak of a cat with falling ears brought from China to Europe by an English sailor toward the end of the 1880s. This little phenomenon awakened interest because up until that moment all the cats of the world had erect ears. It is not possible to affirm whether this Chinese feline had direct descendents, however, other cats with hanging ears were born on a Scottish farm in 1961, which attentive breeders used to create this new singular breed. Although the British and European organizations feel that the folded ear is an undesirable feature that could impair hearing or harbor ear mites, the American and Australian organizations give the Scottish Fold full recognition.

Coat Short hair, dense, soft, and elastic.

Color The range is wide, including most of the American Shorthair colors: white, black, blue, red, cream, smoke, chinchilla, shadeds, torties; also tabby in classic and mackerel variations and bi-color. (See American Shorthair section.)

Body Short, slightly rounded but not large and heavy, compact. Agile legs of medium length.

Head Wide and round on a short and strong neck. The principal distinguishing characteristic of this breed is the position of the ears (small ones preferred), folded forward, giving the animal the likeable appearance of a comical toy or a ceramic figurine. Some breeders consider the folded ears not aesthetically pleasing.

Eyes Round, wide, of a sweet and intense look, divided by a rather large nose. Their color must go with the color of the coat.

Tail Well proportioned, flexible. Some Scottish Folds are born with a large, short tail rounded at the tip; this is considered a fault that excludes it from participation in shows. The fault can be avoided by mating the Scottish Fold with British or American Shorthairs.

Character Home-loving and fond of its master. Apparently peaceable, it is a remarkable mouser and hunter of other small animals.

Ideal owner It becomes very attached to only one person, but shows great affection to all family members.

Environment It is very content to live indoors but likes an occasional escape.

Diet Without problems.

Care Normal brushing. It is a healthy breed, particularly resistant to diseases and to the cold, for which reason winter precautions are not necessary.

Reproduction Only at four weeks of age can it be established whether the kittens will have folded or straight ears.

Faults Thick, short, or kinked tail. Small head or erect ears.

Top: Blue
Bottom: Brown Classic Tabby

Origin The Siamese cat certainly has an Asiatic origin, but it has not been possible to single out the wild species from which it descended. Research in Thailand and Indo-China was fruitless. Old prints, however, show Siamese cats, the first of which we have knowledge, with a striped coat characteristic of wild felines, which demonstrates its provenance from the jungle.

Its introduction into Europe is rather recent. Although mention is made in British cat shows as early as 1871, the King of Siam is supposed to have made a gift of two Siamese to Mr. Owen Gould, English Consul-General in Bangkok, which he took to London in the early 1880s. The following year they made their official appearance at the Crystal Palace in London, where they achieved great success.

Siamese cats reached America in 1890, probably as a gift from the King of Siam to an American friend. They were Siamese of slightly less elegance than those of today. They had cobbier bodies and slightly rounded heads, but they possessed the mysterious charm of the Orient. Unfortunately, because of climate and diverse environments, Siamese proved to be delicate in health.

They became fashionable in the 1920s, and to satisfy the incessant demand for them breeders had to turn out numerous kittens. Because of repeated inbreeding, this beautiful feline became weak and almost extinct. This fear of extinction pressed the breeders to select Siamese with great prudence rather than for mere commercial reasons, resulting in the proud and unpredictable cat that we know today, the most aristocratic exponent of the short-haired breeds.

Coat All Siamese have a close-fitting, short-haired coat, fine textured but thick and glossy.

Color The outstanding feature of the Siamese is its contrasting color pattern called colorpoint. The points are the mask, ears, legs, feet, and tail, and are a rich dark color in contrast to the rest of the body, which is a shade of white. In particular the mask color must visibly join the eyes with tracings to the ears, covering the entire face including the whisker pads but not the top of the head. In North America, only the four basic colors described are considered Siamese. All the other varieties are members of the Colorpoint Shorthair breed. However, the British recognize a number of different Tabby Points, Tortie Tabby Points, Red Points, Tortie Points, and Cream Points as members of the Siamese breed.

Seal Point: This is the most widespread and the earliest Siamese color. The adult is beige, light fawn on the back and almost white on the belly. The mask, ears, legs, feet, and tail are decidedly seal brown; the eyes are blue. All the dark areas must stand out well from the light ground color.

Blue Point: Possesses the same characteristics as the Seal Point, with the difference that the mask, ears, legs, feet, and tail are gray, harmonized well with the ice white of the rest of the coat.

Top: Seal Point
Bottom: Lilac Point

Chocolate Point: Ivory coat with no shading. Points are milk-chocolate color, warm in tone.

Lilac Point: Glacial white coat with gray-pink points and paw pads; the tip of the nose is lavender-pink.

Body Lanky, of medium size, with long, slim hind legs, slightly longer than the forelegs; small, oval feet; good muscle tone; very elegant and haughty movements. The body of the Siamese must be totally devoid of fat.

Head The modern Siamese must have a head shaped in a perfect triangle from the tips of the ears, wide at eye height and tapering to a point toward the chin, with delicate contours. Elongated neck; ears that are wide at the base, ending in points; long and straight nose as a continuation of the forehead.

Eyes Oblique and almond-shaped, inclining toward the nose. A legend tells that the slight squint of the Siamese is due to the fact that they were entrusted with guarding a temple vase of great value; to conscientiously carry out their responsibility they stared at the vase so fixedly that their eyes took on a strange position, but they must never be crossed. Siamese eyes are always a deep, vivid blue.

Tail There are those who assert that a short tail is a sign of Asiatic purity, and those who say that it is a degeneration. The official description is: "Long, thin, tapering to a fine point." According to another legend the curl of the tail is attributed to the princesses of Siam who entrusted their own rings to the cats; these jewels were slipped onto the tails of the Siamese, and in order to avoid their slipping off the cats developed the famous curve in the tail.

Character It is an extremely sensitive and complex cat, sometimes unpredictable in its nervous reactions. From one day to the next, its manner of loving, playing, and general attitude can change radically. Its fickleness gives it a temperament very different from other breeds. It is, however, a genial animal, lively, exuberant, courageous, tamable, jealous, intrusive, and very lovable. Especially when in heat, it meows and howls very impolitely, making sounds similar to those of a newborn baby.

Ideal owner In general it gives its total affection to only one member of the family, even showing indifference to the others. When separated from its master, it is capable of allowing itself to die. Considering its hypersensitive nature, it should be treated by everyone with sweetness. A mature cat is unlikely to tolerate other young cats. But there are cases of successful coexistence.

Environment Lives willingly in an apartment, but dreams of liberty, for which reason it often becomes rambunctious, baring its claws or jumping from one piece of furniture to the other. It needs to burn its energy, therefore if it does not have a fenced in garden, it is necessary to leave the cat free to run about the entire house. It must be watched carefully when in heat, because it will tend to escape.

Diet An excess of food could compromise its figure and therefore its beauty. It would be wise to avoid an exclusively meaty diet, which could bring about an early darkening of the colors of the coat. It is therefore necessary to provide it

Top: Chocolate Point
Bottom: Blue Point

with fish, cooked vegetables, and boiled rice. In the first months of life it must be given vitamin supplements to prevent rickets.

Care Normal daily brushing. A medium-hard brush is needed, which can remove film, dust, and especially all the dead hairs, very numerous during the shedding period.

Reproduction The female reaches puberty earlier than other breeds: she can become pregnant at five months of age and the litters are always large. The kittens at birth are almost white, and the color develops by degrees during their infancy. Though more susceptible to disease than other breeds, the Siamese can live fifteen to twenty years.

Training It is one of the very few breeds that accepts a leash like a dog and can therefore be taken for a walk or on a trip.

Faults Poor health, nasal obstruction or chin malformation, weak legs, eyes which are not blue or squint excessively. Other faults are spots on the belly, too much brown on the head, wide cheeks and short muzzle, excessive sturdiness or thinness, short tail that is hooked, white feet.

Varieties (See Colorpoint Shorthair section for description of other color Siamese cats. See Tonkinese section for a solid-color brown Siamese. See Oriental Shorthair section for other solid-colored Siamese. See Balinese and Javanese sections for long-haired Siamese.)

Blue Point

Origin These native street cats of Singapore have been imported to America very recently and are still very rare. The people of Singapore do not have a particular fondness for cats so the Singapura went relatively unappreciated until foreigners there began to take an interest.

Coat Short, silky, close-lying hair.

Color The only colors seen in America so far are ivory ticked with brown and a bi-color of white and ticked tabby markings. There are many other colors in Singapore.

Body These are small, muscular cats with medium-long legs.

Head Round head with a short nose and a stop. Large, pointed ears and a strong chin.

Eyes Large, open, and slightly slanted.

Tail Medium long with no kinks.

Character A quiet, loving cat.

Ideal owner Patient, quiet people make these cats feel most secure.

Environment Since they have lived on the streets for generations they can adapt to anything, but a quiet apartment is best.

Top: Ivory Ticked with Brown
Bottom: White with Ticked Tabby Markings

Origin   This is a recent, manmade breed that looks like a short-haired Birman. It is sometimes called a Silver Lace because of the white mittens on its dark legs. Because the breed is not generally recognized as yet, the breeding programs differ and there are not established standards. The following is a general description.

Coat   Short, glossy, not too fine.

Color   It has the dark points (mask, ears, legs, and tail) of the Siamese and white mittens on each paw like the Birman.

Seal Point: Fawn coat with dark brown points.

Blue Point: Bluish white coat with dark gray points.

Body   A medium to large, strong cat. It must not resemble the Siamese.

Head   The head forms a triangular shape but should not resemble a Siamese head, which is much more delicate. Large, pointed ears and a stop in the line of the nose.

Eyes   Large, almond-shaped.

Tail   Medium long, not too thin.

Character   An active, loving animal.

Ideal owner   A generally responsible and attentive person who doesn't spend excessive time away from home.

Environment   A spacious apartment with lots of companionship.

Top and bottom: Seal Point

Origin A hairless kitten was born in a normal litter in Canada in 1966, starting the Sphynx breed. This mutation has happened before: in the late 1800s the Mexican Hairless was bred in Mexico.

Coat Very short hair, suedelike on the face, ears, paws, tail, testicles and backbone.

Color The short hair and the skin do reveal coat colors, which can be almost any of the recognized colors.

Body Slender, of light musculature.

Head Not too triangular a shape to the head. A short nose with a stop and large, wide ears. Besides lacking hair, this cat is also whiskerless.

Eyes Golden, green, or hazel.

Tail Long and slim.

Character It is very sociable and affectionate.

Ideal owner This cat lives willingly with any type of family, as long as its owners appreciate and love it.

Environment It must live indoors and in a location that has a temperate climate. The onset of cold weather could cause it to catch serious colds.

Faults Very wrinkled skin or thick down.

Below: Blue
Opposite top: Blue
Opposite bottom: Brown

Origin   It is a North American cross between a Siamese and a Burmese, so it has the visible dark points of the Siamese and the dark coat of the Burmese. This hybrid seems to have captured the best qualities of each.

Coat   Soft, shiny, and close-lying.

Color   These colors have unique names but correspond to the basic Siamese colors.

Natural Mink: Warm brown coat with dark brown points.
Honey Mink: Ruddy brown coat with dark brown points.
Champagne Mink: Beige coat with light brown points.
Blue Mink: Blue-gray coat with slate-blue points.
Platinum Mink: Silver coat with darker silver points.

Body   Medium-sized with long legs. The hind legs are a little longer than the front.

Head   It is moderately triangular with medium-sized, rounded ears. The nose has a slight stop.

Eyes   Almond-shaped, wide-set, blue-green eyes.

Tail   Long and tapering.

Character   This is a very curious, active cat that enjoys company.

Ideal owner   One who can give it all the love and attention that it demands.

Environment   It likes space to exercise. A garden would be appreciated.

Top and bottom: Natural Mink

A GLOSSARY OF CAT CONCERNS

Abandonment   There are more homeless cats than dogs, but the proportion is lower because it is often the cats themselves who choose freedom. The problem of true abandonment arises when, for example, an aged owner dies and his or her family expels the cat, but it is often the saddened pet that runs away. In some countries abandonment of a cat is considered an act of cruelty, punishable by as much as six months in jail.

Abscess   A deposit of pus that may occur in various parts of the animal's body as a reaction to infection. Often abscesses are caused by wounds suffered in fights that become infected by germs from the enemy's claws. They cause a painful swelling, with fever frequently present. An abscess should never be squeezed but brought to a head with localized bathing with warm water and salt. It can be cleaned out with hydrogen peroxide and a cotton-tipped swab.

Acne   A skin disease affecting the chin and the area around the lips. It can be caused by faulty diet, constipation, or hormonal dysfunctions. In light cases, the affected area should be washed with neutral soap and immediately rinsed. In serious cases, including sizable infected areas or the appearance of boils, the services of a veterinarian are required for the administration of antibiotics or surgery.

Aggressiveness   The tendency of a cat to scratch, bite, or bully. Fights between cats are not limited to the mating season but may come about over territorial rights or food. Often aggressive behavior is irreversible and due to psychological disturbances.

Aging   A cat is old at nine years, but its old age can be extended. It will stay at home, wanting only peace and quiet; it will sleep more than before; it will prefer lying in corners away from family activities. Its diet should include less meat and more fish, fresh cheese, and broth, with some fat, but no sweets or tidbits from the table. As it ages, the cat will lose aggressiveness, its sight and hearing will become less acute, it will tend to gain weight, and its bodily functions will be less regular. An aged cat should have a regular checkup by a veterinarian.

Allergy   A state of hypersensitivity to substances normally considered inoffensive—food, medicine, pollen, dust. Symptoms may be swelling, blotching, itching, watering of the eyes, running of the nose, breathing difficulty, pain, digestive upset. Old cats often have food allergies which cause them to scratch themselves and lick their coats. Often a change of diet suffices as a cure. Other allergies affect the respiratory system and cause asthma. The most common allergy among cats is a skin allergy caused by flea bites. The most immediate treatment is to rid the animal of fleas. If the skin is seriously irritated, antiflea medicines and shampoo could aggravate the affliction. The veterinarian should be called. Besides being victims of allergies, cats can also cause them. The mere presence of a cat in a room can cause attacks of asthma or sneezing in many people.

Alopecia   A pathological skin condition resulting in the loss of hair outside the moulting season, with the fur falling out in patches. Avoid home remedies (especially with an alcohol base) and take the cat to a veterinarian immediately.

Anemia   The reduction of red corpuscles in the blood. The seriousness of this complaint depends upon its cause, whether from hemorrhage, insufficient generation of new red corpuscles, infection, etc. Anemia is not a disease but a symptom revealing some pathological development that must be determined. An anemic cat is weak, has a bad appetite, urinates little, wastes away, and develops pallor of the mucous membranes. Once a veterinarian determines the cause of the anemia the cat can be treated properly.

Anesthesia Any gas or drug used to create a state of unconsciousness or insensitivity to pain. A well-equipped veterinary clinic is prepared to administer anesthesia during surgery with the same methods used in hospitals for humans. These include injected muscle relaxants, sedatives, and general anesthetics. Most operations require general anesthesia, from which the animal will quickly recover.

Antibiotics Substances produced from bacteria which can combat harmful microorganisms and their reproduction. The best known antibiotic is penicillin. It should be used only as prescribed by a veterinarian. Prescribed dosages should be followed to the letter.

Arthritis An inflammation of the joints that is often caused by the aging process or exposure to dampness. Older animals are more susceptible than younger ones. X-rays reveal the disease in its various states. Some drugs, such as aspirin, which are beneficial to humans, are harmful to cats. Antipain remedies should be prescribed by a veterinarian.

Ascarids Round worms, cylindrical parasites measuring 1 to 4 in. (2.5 to 10 cm.) in length, pinkish in color, which live in the intestines of cats (and in rare instances also plague humans). Sometimes they are so numerous as to form bundles, which can cause occlusion. Ascarid larvae can be transmitted from a nursing mother cat to its young. It is therefore advisable to have kittens wormed during the first few weeks of life. Worms in an advanced state caused by neglect or ignorance cause loss of weight, swelling of the belly, dullness of the coat, vomiting, convulsions, and progressive weakness. They are life threatening to young kittens. The surest evidence is detection of them in the feces. A veterinarian must prescribe the proper medicine. The cat's environment should be disinfected to destroy all eggs.

Asthma The word means "difficult breathing." It is a chronic disease characterized by labored breathing, coughing spells, and chest constriction. When bronchitis is not treated promptly, it may develop into asthma. In old cats complete recovery is difficult, especially if the cat has heart or lung problems. Limited diet, rest in a dry place, and visits to the veterinarian are necessary.

Bandaging The purpose of bandaging is to stop bleeding or prevent contamination of a wound. Bandaging a wounded cat, however, is difficult, because the cat is nervous, usually in pain, and will try to remove any bandage with its teeth and claws. Applying a wrapped bandage is probably a job for the veterinarian except in an emergency.

Breed A strain or variety of a species of animal, among which aesthetic and psychological qualities are transmitted from one generation to another in a highly selective manner.

Bronchitis Inflammation of the bronchial tubes, of which the symptoms are depression, chills, coughing, and loss of appetite. The most common kind of bronchitis is caused by respiratory diseases. Treatment is to keep the cat in a room at constant temperature and to give it expectorants. Chronic bronchitis is a typical disease of old cats. Such cases are mostly treated by the giving of expectorants and sedatives in an effort to avoid the development of asthma. A serious complication is bronchial pneumonia, which is particularly grave because the infection attacks the lung tissue. The cat appears depressed, has a dry cough, high fever, quickened breathing, and loss of appetite with increased thirst. The services of a veterinarian are absolutely necessary. Drugs and antibiotics may bring about recovery in two weeks, but the cat will need a period of convalescence in a dry place, with a light diet of foods particularly to its liking.

Burns   The most common types of burns are those from heated objects or from boiling water. Often the seriousness of the injury is underestimated because no welts are visible on the cat's skin and the fur is undisturbed. But if the hair comes out easily when pulled it means that the burn is serious and must be treated immediately. While waiting for the veterinarian's examination, one can relieve pain by applying ice or cold compresses to the burn. Electrical burns may happen when a cat is playing with a lamp cord or similar device. The shock is most frequently sustained by the mouth, but the veterinarian should check to see whether there is any damage to the lungs.

Cesarean birth   The method by which kittens are delivered by surgical means through the abdominal wall. Cesarean births are sometimes advisable for small females, which are constitutionally unable to cope with normal birth.

Caries   The result of deterioration of the enamel of the teeth with the formation of cavities. The problem in cats usually is noticed when the animal suffers while chewing. Sometimes bad breath is also a symptom. The veterinarian can decide whether or not the ailing tooth should be extracted; the operation should take place with anesthesia.

Castration   The surgical removal of the testicles of the male cat. Altering should be performed after the sixth or seventh month or when the vet advises. To avoid obesity, altered cats should not be overfed.

Cataract   An eye disease which attacks older cats. The crystalline lens of the eye becomes opaque and vision is sharply reduced. Causes may be diabetes, poisoning, traumas, or old age. Surgery is recommended, especially if the animal is young.

Cat registration   Genealogical listing of all purebred cats with their detailed pedigrees. Every cat fanciers' association keeps such a record of all members' animals. A cat must be entered in the files before a pedigree is issued.

Cattery   The place where breeders mate cats with the aim of maintaining the purity and perfection of a breed and to supply kittens for sale.

Clubs   Cat clubs organize breeders, exhibitors, judges, and owners of a given breed. Other duties include formulation and revision of the standards and promotion of perfection of the breed. The cat clubs are not the same as associations. They are localized with no overall mission such as registering kittens, etc.

Colic   A morbid syndrome with acute abdominal pain connected with disease, the swallowing of foreign bodies, or fecal impaction. Diagnosis and treatment must be made by a veterinarian. The use of laxatives should be avoided.

Constipation   Difficulty in bowel movement. When it occurs, a change in diet is recommended (fresh liver, for example, has a laxative effect), together with the administration of a spoonful of vaseline oil or corn oil. Constipation may be caused at times by the cat's swallowing hair. If the condition is serious and persistent, surgery may be necessary.

244

Contusion   The result of a violent blow from a noncutting outside object (collision, fall, a thrown stone, etc.), usually accompanied by painful swelling. There may be lacerations, bruises, or hematoma (a swelling suffused with blood). The blood is normally reabsorbed quickly upon application of a warm poultice or a pomade.

Cystitis   Inflammation of the bladder caused by bacteria. Urination becomes frequent and difficult, and the urine is clouded by albumin or pus. The attack is accompanied by fever and pains. Antibiotics offer a quick cure. There should always be a dish of fresh water so that the cat is free to drink as often as it wishes. The litter box should be kept as clean as possible.

Dandruff   A healthy cat should have a soft skin free from scabs and dandruff. If dandruff is present, it is a possible sign of fleas, tapeworm, allergic dermatitis, or some other ailment. Consult a veterinarian.

Deafness   A cat's ears may be afflicted by hardening of the duct, accumulation of wax, perforation of the eardrum, catarrh—all disturbances which can lead to deafness.

Dermatitis   Inflammation of the skin caused by parasites, infection, or allergy, which the cat may try to relieve by scratching.

Diabetes   A disease mostly of old cats caused by faulty diet, obesity, genetic factors, or reaction to some drugs. The animal loses weight, drinks an unusual amount of water, urinates frequently, and is weak. Diagnosis is through urine analysis. Treatment is with insulin and diet control.

Digitalis   A heart tonic sometimes prescribed in small doses to strengthen the heartbeat.

Disinfestation   The process by which harmful parasites infesting the cat are destroyed. Baths and antiparasite powders are useful. Fleas reproduce in tight corners of the animal's bed and on the adjacent floor. Thus a thorough cleaning is needed in the area where the cat has its bed.

Distemper   *See* Feline infectious enteritis.

Drugs   Drugs used in veterinary medicine are specially formulated for cats; sometimes they are the same as those used for humans. They must, of course, be prescribed carefully to avoid overdoses with harmful results.

Dysentery   An infection of the lower intestinal tract causing pain, fever, and severe diarrhea. It may come from a number of causes: faulty diet, colds, feline enteritis, intestinal parasites, poisoning or other gastrointestinal afflictions. The cat should be kept in a warm room without eating, and the veterinarian should be called.

Dyspnea   Labored breathing following accidents or during pulmonary afflictions. The cause must be determined immediately and treatment undertaken.

Eczema   Inflammation of the skin with reddening, formation of vesicles, and/or scabs. The cat aggravates the condition by scratching. The various types of eczema can be caused by food poisoning, bad skin care, abnormal liver function, vitamin deficiency, or allergy. The complaint may be acute or chronic and may attack various parts of the body, especially the back and tail, the neck and the head. A veterinarian may give injections to guard against liver damage and apply suitable ointments after bathing the affected area. Diet should be changed to include fish, fresh cheeses, buttermilk, or yogurt.

Enteritis   Intestinal inflammation from toxic causes (food poisoning, long-term constipation) or from bacterial infection. Mild cases are treated with twenty-four hours of fasting followed by a diet of skim milk and broths.

More severe cases, accompanied by fever, will call for administration of antispasmodics and/or antibiotics. Infectious enteritis is a contagious disease which, if not quickly diagnosed, may be fatal. It can be prevented by vaccination.

Estrus Pertaining to the periods of ovulation in female cats. Referred to as "being in heat."

Euthanasia Death intentionally caused, most often by injection of drugs that cause cessation of heart action. It is used to "put to sleep" pets which may have an incurable disease and to spare them useless suffering.

Exercise Docile cats or those who are kept indoors become fat and flabby and have less resistance to fatigue and illness. Thus exercise is a necessity. The problem does not exist for cats that have a yard to run in, but for indoor cats the owner should give them a chance to exercise through play.

Eyes An owner should examine the cat's eyes often and, when necessary, clean them with a little cotton dampened with lukewarm water. Cat's eyes can be harmed by dust, cold drafts, lesions, or foreign bodies, which may lead to conjunctivitis, corneal ulceration, or cataracts. Any of these afflictions left untended may result in blindness.

Fatigue City cats, for example, when taken to the country, may suffer from fatigue caused by overdoing their physical activity. They may appear depressed, indifferent, and may vomit or have blood in their urine. Total rest is the proper cure.

Fear The instinct for self-preservation leads unattached cats to avoid humans, dogs, loud noises, and strange places. A housecat, however, is normally much more relaxed, and even if frightened by some unexpected event can usually be easily quieted. Abnormal cases of inborn, or congenital, timidity are hard to remedy.

Feline infectious enteritis (also called panleucopenia) This disease is caused by a virus and is fatal, particularly in kittens and young cats, if not treated immediately by a vet. The symptoms are listlessness, loss of appetite, vomiting, extraordinary thirst, rise of temperature and rapid deterioration in condition. If a kitten is vomiting and looks poorly, call the vet immediately. Speed is essential. All kittens should be vaccinated against feline infectious enteritis, usuallly at about ten to twelve weeks.

Feline respiratory diseases These include rhinotracheitis (FVR), calicivirus (FC I), feline pneumonitis (FPN), feline reovirus infection (FRI), and felinae syncytia-forming viruses (FSV). These are all referred to as upper respiratory infection (URI), which are similar in effect and means of transmission. These highly contagious viruses are usually spread through the air and cause intense sneezing and inflammation. A diligent vaccination program administered by a veterinarian is helpful in preventing URI. Without veterinary attention, death is likely, especially among kittens, aging, and stressed cats.

Fever A cat's normal temperature range is 100.5° to 102.5°F. The animal is feverish, sad, has little appetite, and stays by itself—all symptoms of some complaint which must be diagnosed.

Foreign bodies Such foreign bodies as slivers, fish bones, or other pointed bones may get stuck in the cat's throat or gums. If the cat does not succeed in removing such bodies by its own efforts, the services of a veterinarian may be required.

Fracture Fractures are of two types—simple, when there is no visible break in the skin, and compound, when a bone protrudes from a wound. Deformations of the legs as a result of a fracture may be apparent, the animal's movements may be abnormal, or the legs may be unable to sustain the cat's weight. Usually the pet cries out continually. The veterinarian should treat all fractures. It is best *not* to apply a splint yourself.

Gastritis   An irritation of the stomach caused by indigestion, spoiled food, chills, or vermin. A symptom is the vomiting of a clear or yellow fluid in an effort to rid its body of harmful food. Fasting for twenty-four hours is recommended. There is also an acute form of gastritis with not only vomiting but also high fever, diarrhea, and excessive thirst. In such cases a visit to the veterinarian is absolutely necessary.

Gingivitis   Inflammation of the gums caused by tartar on the teeth, spoiled foods, medicines not tolerated by the cat, or tooth cavities. There may be swelling, bleeding, and pus. Treatment is by local disinfection.

Heart, diseases of   The four major categories of heart disease are congestive heart failure, pre-heart failure states, arrhythmia, and shock with hypertension. Old cats are most likely to suffer. The most apparent symptoms are difficult breathing, trembling, and excessive fatigue. Care of a veterinarian is absolutely essential.

Heatstroke   Extremely hot, humid weather may cause heatstroke in cats if they are not kept cool and given ample water. Symptoms include elevated body temperature (110°F.), suffering, staggering, possible vomiting and collapse. The cat should be removed immediately to a cool place, where ice compresses should be applied. Blood circulation can be improved by body massage. A cat must never be left in a closed car exposed to the sun, nor should it be required to travel for long distances during unusually hot weather. Very young kittens are especially vulnerable to heatstroke, as are old cats and overweight animals.

Hemorrhage   Continuous loss of blood from a wound or lesion which results from the breaking of veins or arteries. The bleeding should be stopped as quickly as possible by cold compacts and pressure on the wound. Surgery is often required. If the bleeding is from an artery, use of a tourniquet above the wound is necessary. Lesions caused by being hit by a car or other vehicle may cause internal hemorrhaging in which blood accumulates in the abdomen, stomach, or bladder. The animal must be permitted absolute rest under the care of a vet.

Heredity   The transmission of physical and psychological characteristics from parents to offspring. The extension of characteristics from one generation to another is not all inclusive, since the young may all resemble the father, or all may resemble the mother, or half may resemble one parent and the remaining half the other, thus transmitting traits from distant ancestors as well.

Hydrophobia (rabies)   A very serious disease that may strike dogs, wolves, mice, and cats. The rabies virus can be transmitted by the bite of an infected animal. A victim of rabies seeks the dark, is irritable, tries to hide, is given to unprovoked scratching, and is unable to drink because of paralysis of the glottis. Death is certain. Cats rarely catch the disease, because they are not likely to come in contact with an infected cat and because the disease is becoming rare. It is still a good idea to have the cat vaccinated against rabies, particularly if it lives in a region where rabies has been reported, especially among mice.

Hygiene   All the activities aimed at cleanliness of the animal's body, such as combing, brushing, elimination of parasites, bathing and dry shampooing, proper diet, and regularity of bowel movements.

Indigestion Caused by overfeeding, faulty diet, voracious eating, swallowing foreign bodies, gastritis, and other factors. The cat seems depressed, refuses to eat, suffers from stomach pains, and whines; it may even seem to be undergoing a nervous attack. A brief period without eating is usually enough to bring the animal back to normal form. Regular eating should be resumed gradually, starting with broth.

Infection Sickness caused by penetration of germs into the body, where they reproduce. A cat's wounds, especially if it lives much of its life outdoors, can easily become infected. If neglected or badly treated, infections can worsen into abscesses.

Influenza Symptoms include sneezing, discharge of fluid from the eyes, loss of appetite, fever, ulcers on tongue, drooling, and apathy. If properly treated, the cat should be cured in a week or ten days, but if neglected influenza may open the way for serious viral disease. Even a simple cold is reason enough to keep the cat in a warm place, well protected from dampness and drafts.

Injection The process by which liquid medicines are put into some part of the body. It may be subcutaneous or hypodermic, when simply directed beneath the skin. The best place on a cat's body is the flank adjacent to the kidneys after the skin has been caught up into a fold by the operator's fingers. When giving an animal injections, it is a good plan for one or two family members to hold it down, because it will struggle to escape the needle.

Insect bites Such bites become noticeable when there is swelling around the bite. If an insect stinger is visible, it should be removed with tweezers. If the stinger is not visible and swelling continues, with or without respiratory complications, the cat should be taken to the veterinarian.

Laryngitis Inflammation of the larynx, often in association with pharyngitis. Symptoms are tickling of the throat, coughing, hoarseness. The affliction appears after a cold or an attack of influenza.

Laxative Medication for the relief of constipation. Emollients used in the preparation of typical laxatives include mineral oil or petroleum jelly (1 tsp. in the food for two or three days). Laxatives should be used only on the advice of the veterinarian.

Licking If a cat persists in licking a given part of its body, it probably means that it has a wound, foreign body, or perhaps an abscess is forming. The owner should examine the localized area to ascertain what the problem is. Licking, however, is a normal technique of self-grooming and is quite normal when not obsessively confined to one area of the body.

Limping When a cat limps or keeps one leg uplifted while walking, it means it has had an accident. The vet will be able to ascertain whether it is caused by a bruise, twisting of the leg, dislocation, or fracture.

Loss of appetite Whenever a cat that has always eaten normally loses its appetite, the owner should be alerted, since it may be symptomatic of indigestion, feline infectious enteritis or cat flu, a cold, or fever. If the condition lasts for several days and signs of weight loss appear, then treatment by a veterinarian should be arranged.

Mange A disease caused by the presence of parasitic mites barely visible to the naked eye. There are several varieties of mites, each attacking different sections of the body. Otodectes cynotis live in the ear canal, causing dark wax which in turn itches the cat persistently. Notoedres cati are mites that localize on the head by burrowing beneath the skin, causing itching and loss of hair. Trombiculid mites (chiggers) can land on any part of the body. They are red, orange, or yellowish specks no bigger than the point on a pin. They cause severe itching. All mites must be treated by a veterinarian with a form of insecticide formulated for cats plus a topical treatment for relief of the symptoms.

Mastitis Acute inflammation of the nipples in a nursing female cat. It is caused by a trauma, infection, or blocked passage of the milk through the mammary glands. Symptoms are swelling or hardening of the nipples, which may also become fevered or purplish, possibly with the emission of discolored milk that may be streaked with blood. The affliction may strike only one nipple. Hot compresses applied to the area may give relief until the animal can be seen by the veterinarian.

Metritis An infection of the uterus that may appear after birth of a litter in case of lack of hygiene or retention of the afterbirth. The mother cat is depressed, taking little interest in the kittens, and has a serous discharge. The affliction is treated with local irrigation and antibiotics. Normally cats suffering from metritis do not produce sufficient milk for feeding the litter or the milk may be toxic, and it is necessary to feed the kittens artificially.

Miscarriage The death of unborn kittens can be natural, provoked, or accidental. Natural miscarriage may come about because of lack of irrigation of the placenta, infection of the uterine mucous membrane, rejection (the fetus is a foreign body), or congenital defects. It is voluntary, or provoked, when an unwanted pregnancy is terminated by the veterinarian (within two weeks of mating). Accidental miscarriage may be caused by a fall, a kick, or a blow by a moving vehicle.

Nephritis Inflammation of the kidneys resulting from a severe illness that overtaxes the kidneys. In the acute form of nephritis, the animal suffers from depression, colic, painful and increased urination, thirst, vomiting, or loss of appetite. Urinalysis is the key to accurate diagnosis. If neglected, this disease can be fatal.

Neurosis Strong emotions, toxic reactions, and extended sickness can cause a cat to become neurotic, with changes in humor and behavior, onset of fears and constant mewing. The cause(s) of the neurosis should be eliminated and treatment begun to remedy the animal's condition.

Obesity Overweightness is harmful to joints, the heart, and the lungs. The obese cat becomes lethargic. Overweightness is almost always caused by overeating. A low-calorie diet with vitamin and mineral supplements should be started and strictly adhered to.

Otitis Inflammation of the outer ear. It becomes reddened, there is an excessive flow of wax, and the cat tends to scratch its ear more than normally. Regular cleansing of the ear can prevent the onset of otitis, which is encouraged by the presence of eczema, mange mites, or foreign bodies. If untended, otitis may lead to deafness.

Paralysis An affliction in which abnormalities in the nervous system lead to partial or total loss of sensation in certain parts of the body. In cats paralysis can be caused by calcium deficiency, which leads in turn to decalcification of the bones, fractures, a broken spinal column with lesions in the spinal cord, or by a cerebral hemorrhage. Immediate treatment is necessary.

Parasites Creatures that live upon others, often causing discomfort or disease. Parasites that take up residence on the cat's skin include fleas, ticks, and lice, which can be eliminated by the use of powders, certain compresses, or pesticide collars. Internal parasites invade the cat's stomach, intestine, or blood stream. These include roundworms, hookworms, heartworms, protozoans, strongyloides, and tapeworms. Tests, including micro-examination of the feces, can determine whether a cat is free from or afflicted by parasites. Left untreated, internal and external parasites weaken the animal, leaving it more susceptible to disease.

Pedigree The cat's family tree as attested by a document that lists a pet's maternal and paternal ancestors. The source documents are the registration files of breeders' associations. When buying a purebred cat, an owner is entitled to a pedigree.

Pleurisy Inflammation of the pleura, which is the serous membrane surrounding the lung. Causes include: deep wounds in the thorax, severe colds, bronchial pneumonia, tuberculosis. The cat finds breathing painful, has a dry cough, and a slight fever. It should be taken to a veterinarian for treatment.

Pneumonia An acute virus infection of the lungs caused by a severe cold in a weak animal. It is often associated with bronchitis and pleurisy. Symptoms include high fever, dry cough, difficulty in breathing, loss of appetite. The disease attacks young cats particularly. Treatment by the veterinarian includes injections of antibiotics and the administration of expectorants. Convalescence in a warm environment takes about one month.

Poisoning May be caused by spoiled food, poisoned meat set out to destroy pests, mice killed by arsenic, household or garden chemicals, or poisons cruelly fed to the animal by others. Other household poisons are lead, petroleum distilates, detergents, lye, cleansers, mothballs, and medications such as aspirin. It is almost never possible to notice poisoning at the moment it occurs but only later, when the symptoms become evident. Such symptoms include heavy flow of saliva, a sense of suffocation, diarrhea, collapse, and nervous attacks. The animal should be taken to the veterinarian as quickly as possible.

Prognosis Forecast of the eventual course of a disease. It may be (1) "good," if it looks forward to healing; (2) "guarded," if the outcome is unsure; or (3) "poor," if a cure appears impossible.

Prophylaxis A term indicating the rules followed to prevent or avoid disease; preventive medicine.

Pyometra A uterine infection which attacks aged female cats (usually unspayed who have never had a litter). Symptoms are listlessness, lack of appetite, great thirst, and frequent urination. Odorous discharge is common. Treatment calls for ovariohysterectomy.

Pyorrhea (periodontitis) A disease of the gums surrounding the teeth resulting in eventual loss of a tooth if not treated. The affliction is found chiefly in old cats. Symptoms are hesitancy to chew hard food, also bleeding gums. Treatment is removal of plaque and/or tartar.

Quarantine Period during which an animal is isolated in an effort to avoid the spreading of disease. Some countries impose quarantine on imported cats and dogs for no less than six months particularly to prevent the introduction of rabies.

Rabies *See* Hydrophobia.

Respiratory ailments The first symptom of respiratory illness is sneezing followed by watering of the eyes, listlessness, and loss of appetite. If the breathing rate increases or there is fever, attention by the veterinarian is required. The complaint may prove serious in the case of old animals with heart problems, but in most cases treatment with antibiotics is sufficient, especially if diagnosis has been prompt.

Rheumatism A localized or spreading pain in the muscles, joints, and associated structures possibly due to exposure to cold and dampness. The animal whines and tends to limp. Most of the time the acute form of the disease will clear up in about a week. Chronic forms are long-lasting and painful. The cat should live in dry surroundings, carefully dried if it comes into the house with a wet coat, and care should be taken to ensure that it does not sleep on cold floors. Rheumatism is a general term for various related diseases such as rheumatoid arthritis, rheumatic fever, or osteoarthritis.

Rickets A disease that attacks the skeleton, resulting in deformations thereof. Symptoms of rickets appear especially in young cats as the result of an insufficient amount of vitamin D or defective diet. In kittens it results in crooked legs and curvature of the spine. Spontaneous fractures and a tendency to pick up diseases may characterize an animal with rickets. In treatment and prevention the diet should include milk, soft cheeses, minerals, and vitamin D in addition to meat. An all-meat diet creates an imbalance in the calcium/phosphorous ratio. However, there is more danger in *overdosing* vitamin D. Consult a veterinarian. In adult animals, although the effect of rickets remains, it is possible to strengthen the skeleton.

Ringworm A highly contagious skin disease caused not by a worm, but a fungus. it appears in patches, frequently growing from the center outward in a ring pattern. It may show up under an ultraviolet light. A vet will prescribe suitable treatment. Gloves should always be worn when handling an animal with suspected ringworm, as it is also very contagious to humans.

Scurvy A disease caused by a deficiency of vitamin C. It may strike cats that have had deficient diets and strays at all ages. A symptom is the ease with which blood vessels break; sometimes there is ulceration of the gums and anemia. Treatment is by a diet rich in vitamin C (raw liver, milk, vegetables, vitamin C supplements) and medicines as prescribed by the veterinarian.

Self-care When a cat is feeling sick, it may try to cure itself by fasting (for stomach problems), vomiting (if it has consumed poison), eating grass, licking open wounds to bathe them in saliva, or simply seeking out a private spot if it simply needs quiet. This kind of self-therapy is always useful in the case of minor complaints.

Shedding At the beginning of hot weather a cat replaces its old hair with summer growth. If there is excessive loss of hair or if bare spots are left on the skin, the animal may be suffering from eczema, dermatitis, or parasite infection. Daily brushing is especially important during the moulting period. Many house cats shed continuously, which may be normal for them.

Shows Cat shows take place around the world, in which owners show their animals, provided they are registered with an association and thus in possession of a pedigree. There are judges expert in each breed. They apply the official standards rigidly, examining competing cats in regard to color, pattern, and texture of coat, body conformation, dentition, eye color, ears, etc. Thus each cat is given a score, and from its record over a number of showings may win the title of Champion or Grand Champion.

Standard A set of descriptions fixed by a given cat fanciers' association for each breed. Official standards describe height and length, coat color and pattern, consistency of fur, eye color, shape of head and muzzle, character, etc. In the United States there are seven cat registry organizations, each with its own set of breeds and standards.

Stomatitis Inflammation of the mucous membrane of the mouth. It may be caused by too hot food, gingivitis, or infectious disease. The cat tends to stay by itself, exhibits increased thirst, salivates excessively, and eats unwillingly. Treatment must be under the care of a veterinarian.

Symptoms Alarming symptoms that should move the owner to investigate include: persistent constipation, diarrhea, frequent urination, coughing, loss of weight, limping, discharge from the nose or eyes, sneezing, tangled fur, dullness of coat, loss of appetite, listlessness.

Tail The shape, length, and thickness of the tail are important elements in the overall beauty of a cat. The tail also acts as a kind of rudder, helping the cat to keep its balance. Movements of the tail are used to gauge a cat's various emotional states and attitudes.

Tartar A yellowish-brown material that sometimes covers the base of the teeth. Inflammation of the gums may lurk under such an incrustation, or it may be a symptom of weakening of the roots, the presence of an abscess, causing bad breath. Tartar should be removed by the veterinarian with proper instruments; sometimes anesthesia is required. If trained from kittenhood, most cats will allow cleaning of the teeth with a small, rough brush.

Thirst Cats are not great drinkers normally, and so any increased thirst is noticeable. Such craving for water may indicate diseases of the digestive system, viral infections, diabetes, or fever.

Tranquilizers Should be given to cats only on responsible medical advice. Otherwise there may be bad reactions, such as lowering of blood pressure and collapse. A veterinarian may prescribe a mild tranquilizer before travel or minor surgery.

Tumor Abnormal tissue growth in an organism, progressive and usually tending to get worse. There are tumors of the viscera, skin, and nervous centers. Old cats are especially likely to get tumors. Benign tumors can be removed by surgery and do not return. Malignant tumors tend to spread even after the basic tumor has been removed by surgery.

Ulcer A small lesion formed in the stomach or intestine and caused by ingestion of corrosive substances, gastroenteritis, stomatitis, presence of parasites. Symptoms: loss of appetite, vomiting, diarrhea, depression, nervous manifestations, and expressions of pain. Ulcers must be treated by the veterinarian.

Underweight Usually caused by lack of sufficiently abundant food or by malfunctions of the nutritive process. If a cat has a good appetite but still loses weight, this is symptomatic of illness, and the animal should be examined by a veterinarian. If a cat has lost weight because of being deprived of food, its normal diet should be restored gradually.

Urination Sometimes a cat, whether male or female, may spray its urine on a wall rather than on the ground or in the litter box. This is instinctive behavior—pertaining to territory-claiming and sexual messages to other cats. If this action of spraying continues for several days, it may be a symptom of trouble in the animal's urinary system. Cats can also be stricken with urolithiasis, which are tiny stones that obstruct the urinary canal and press against the urethra. When urination is blocked in this way, the excessive retention of toxic wastes that are normally eliminated by the kidneys may cause incurable damage.

Usual Term used by British Cat Fancy, meaning coat color most often shown with respect to a specific breed.

Vaccination At an early age determined by a veterinarian all cats should be vaccinated against several upper respiratory diseases, feline infectious enteritis (panleukopenia) and rabies.

Virus Organisms smaller than bacteria and invisible under ordinary microscopes. They multiply only on living tissue and are the cause of many infectious diseases. Some cancers are suspected of viral origins.

Vitamins An organic compound necessary for the processing of nutrition; they are essential to the growth and basic health of a cat. Besides vitamin complexes, cats get most useful vitamins from such raw foods as meat, eggs, vegetables, and milk. Commercial cat foods labeled as "complete" or "balanced" usually supply the daily vitamin and mineral requirements of normal cats. Consult a veterinarian.

Vitamin and mineral supplements Fresh foods are a natural source for all vitamins and minerals. Because it is impossible to know with any certainty whether a given cat is receiving its daily requirement many cat-owners use a high-quality vitamin and mineral supplement in pill, liquid, or powder form. Because this subject causes intense debate within the veterinary community itself the cat-owner must make a subjective decision based on his or her own beliefs. Talk to several veterinarians, breeders, and other experienced fanciers.

Vomiting The forced expulsion of the contents of the stomach through the mouth. Vomiting is not a disease but a symptom of a disease or discomfort. Often it is caused by eating spoiled food, plastic, grass, paper, bones, or cloth. If vomiting continues, the cat should be kept without food and taken to a veterinarian.

Water In the wild, cats drink no more than every twenty-four hours, but there should always be a dish of clean water available so that a house pet's needs are satisfied. A cat can go long periods without eating, but a total lack of water soon results in dehydration. In case of stomach ailments, the quantity of water should be limited.

Watering of the eyes Irritation of the eyes of cats causes tears to form. Causes include conjunctivitis, wounding of the cornea, obstruction of the tear canals, and allergy. Excessive tearing may be caused by an infection of the primary respiratory system. In long-haired breeds, watering of the eyes may be the result of a tickling irritation caused by the hairs. The eye area should be bathed frequently and the hairs should be trimmed.

Wounds and sores Breaks in the skin with alteration of the connective tissues. Wounds are almost invariably inflicted from outside sources; they should be disinfected with hydrogen peroxide and then treated with antibiotics in emulsion or powder form. Wounds that do not mend readily should be sutured by a veterinarian.

X-rays They should be made if the cat is suffering from a fracture, kidney stones, foreign bodies in the stomach or intestine, etc. There are special X-ray machines for handling cats and dogs.

BIBLIOGRAPHY

Catcott, E.J., DVM, Ph.D. *Feline Medicine & Surgery*. Second Edition. Santa Barbara, California: American Veterinary Publications, Inc., 1975.

Gebhardt, R.H., Pond, G. and Raleigh, Dr. I. *A. Standard Guide to Cat Breeds*. New York: Mc Graw-Hill Book Company, 1979.

Ing, C. and Pond, G. *Champion Cats of the World*. London: Harrap & Co. Ltd., 1972.

Kirk, R. W., BS, DVM. *First Aid for Pets*. New York: A Sunrise Book E.P. Dutton, 1978.

Leyhausen, P. *Cat Behavior*. New York: Garland STPM Press, 1979.

Loxton, H. *Spotter's Guide to Cats*. London: Usborne Publishing Ltd.

Loxton, H. and Warner, P. *Guide to the Cats of the World*. Oxford, England: Elsevier Phaidon/Phaidon Press Ltd., 1975.

Montgomery, J. *The World of Cats*. London: Hamlyn Publishing Group Ltd., 1972.

Pugnetti, G. *Guida al gatto. La storia, le razze, come allevarlo e curarlo*. Milano, Italy: Mondadori, 1978.

Shook Hazen, B. *The Concise Encyclopedia of Cats*. New York: Octopus/Vineyard Books, Inc., 1974.

Siegal, M. *The Good Cat Book*. New York: Simon & Schuster, Inc., 1981.

Warner, M. *Cats of the World*. New York: The Ridge Press/Bantam Books, Inc., 1976.

Wright, M., Walters, S., Stein, B. S. and Thompson, S. R. *The Book of the Cat*. New York: Summit Books, 1980.

INDEX OF ENTRIES

PICTURE CREDITS